Diary of My Travels in America

DIARY OF MY TRAVELS IN AMERICA

Louis-Philippe, King of France, 1830-1848

Translated from the French by Stephen Becker • Preface by Henry Steele Commager

Delacorte Press/New York

Published by
Delacorte Press
1 Dag Hammarskjold Plaza
New York, N.Y. 10017

Originally published in French by Librairie Ernest Flammarion under the title
Journal de Mon Voyage d'Amérique. Copyright © 1976 by Flammarion.
English translation copyright © 1977 by Dell Publishing Co., Inc.

Preface copyright © 1977 by Henry Steele Commager

Manufactured in the United States of America
First U.S.A. printing

Designed by Giorgetta Bell McRee

LIBRARY OF CONGRESS CATALOGING IN PUBLICATION DATA

Louis-Philippe, King of the French, 1773–1850.
  Diary of my travels in America.

  Translation of Journal de mon voyage d'Amérique.
  1. United States—Description and travel—1783–1848.
  2. Louis-Philippe, King of the French, 1773–1850.
  I. Title.
  E164.L6813   917.4'04'3   77–23955
          ISBN 0–440–01844–7

Contents

Preface

by Henry Steele Commager

From the first discoveries by Columbus and his successors, America fascinated the Old World. Where had it been all these years since the expulsion from the Garden (5496 years by Bishop Usher's careful computations); why had it come so long so late on the stage of history; why had God chosen to conceal it so long from his own people? Was it really a new world, a special creation? How to account for its savage state, for its flora and fauna so unlike anything known in the Old World, for the miasmal swamps and the vast territories locked in eternal ice; how to account for the venomous reptiles, the poisonous insects, the savages (half men, half beasts), the absence, after all these centuries, of any real civilization? Even before these questions were fully answered, America presented a new and more serious galaxy of questions. For by the eighteenth century all had changed. Now the English in America had thrown off their colonial yoke and—for the first time in history—brought forth a new nation. They had drafted the first written constitutions, set up the first federal system, instituted the first system of self-government—what had they not done? The earlier mystery of America was still there (especially for the vast continent to the south); to it was now added new and even more importunate subjects for inquiry.

No wonder visitors swarmed over from the Old World to the New to see for themselves what it was like, and what it portended for the future. In a broad sense, they came either as interpreters or as reporters—interpreters who inquired anxiously into the character of America and the implications of the American experiment for the Old World, and reporters who merely wanted to see for themselves, or to excite—and perhaps profit from—the curiosity of their countrymen about what was, in fact, a novel spectacle: oddly enough, the novelty never seemed to wear off. Among the first were a number of distinguished Frenchmen—Crèvecoeur *(The American Farmer)*, de Tocqueville, Michel Chevalier, in the early years; Maurois, Siegfried, and Daniel Aron in our own time. It is clearly to this second category —those who mostly wanted to satisfy their own curiosity—that young Louis-Philippe belongs. And in his case, as with Georges Clemenceau seventy years later, our interest is not only in what he observed, but in the observer himself, for this young adventurer of twenty-four was to be the king of the French.

Louis-Philippe was a voluntary observer, but an involuntary visitor. He was, like so many of his countrymen who had fled either the Revolution in France or the slave uprising in Santo Domingo, a refugee. He had tried, briefly, to accommodate himself to the Revolution: as a lad of eighteen he had joined the Jacobin Club in Paris; he had enlisted in the army and was promptly made a lieutenant general, and fought for his country against the Austrian invaders. Then, alas, he listened to his commanding general, Dumouriez, and went over to the enemy. From that moment on he was in flight. He took refuge in Switzerland, where he taught mathematics at a provincial academy; he wandered through the Germanies, into Denmark and Norway; he visited Lapland and lived with the Lapps—a preparation, as it turned out, for his later adventures with the Cherokees in Tennessee; he was feted by the king of Sweden. He was potentially a danger, and the Directory wanted him out of the way: they offered to free his

2

younger brothers, the Duc de Montpensier and the Comte de Beaujolais, from their dungeon in Marseilles, if they would all betake themselves to America. Louis-Philippe had no money, but the American minister in Paris, Gouverneur Morris, took care of that, and in the fall of 1796, armed with a Danish passport, the young Frenchman sailed to the New World. Within a few months his brothers followed—a Swedish ship, this time, bearing eighty Americans rescued from Algerian captivity. They met in Philadelphia, in time to witness the inauguration of John Adams to the presidency.

Philadelphia was exciting enough; if it was not quite Paris or London, it was the American Edinburgh, the American Weimar, the political capital of the new nation; the social, the financial, the religious, the cultural as well. Louis-Philippe leased a house for his royal family and his one retainer, the faithful valet, Beaudoin. He involved himself in the social whirl of the little capital, he paid court (so it is said) to the dashing Miss Willing, daughter of the leading banker of the city, who discouraged the match with the sagacious observation that if Louis-Philippe's position did not improve, he was not good enough for the girl, and if it did, she was not good enough for him! And he decided to see America.

So off they went, the four of them, with a few thousand dollars (borrowed) in their purses, a couple of horses, and a romantic curiosity. They found their way to the new city of Washington, still very much in embryo. They admired Georgetown, they sailed down the Potomac to Mount Vernon to pay their respects to General Washington, now retired from the presidency, and they could doubtless

3

reflect that retirement from the throne in the Old World was not quite so agreeable. Washington drew up an ambitious itinerary for them, and they were off, in the soft spring, for a great swing through Virginia and into the remote frontier of Tennessee and Kentucky, to the Great Lakes, to New York, to New England, eventually to New Orleans. What an odyssey.

We can accompany the royal family through only the first part of their travels, for though "Mr. Orleans," as he was known, kept diaries of them all, only the first has survived; we do have, by good fortune, Montpensier's watercolors—or lithographs of them, almost miraculously preserved. No need to comment on the comments of Louis-Philippe, and as for Montpensier's paintings, M. Babelon has dealt with those. What interests us is rather the impact of the new United States on the mind of this romantic young aristocrat—an aristocrat, withal, who confessed deep bourgeois instincts. What was it that struck him most powerfully?

First, he saw a people on the move—on the move physically, socially, and economically. He had come from a society where change could be brought about only by revolution and violence; he found one where change was the order of the day, not only taken for granted but welcomed. The Duke's father had been called Égalité (that did not save him from the guillotine), but if you wanted true equality—among whites anyway—you had to come to the New World and, once there, to the frontier. Louis-Philippe enjoyed Philadelphia society, but he did not bother to record it; what impressed him was the west, the frontier. He saw, as Crèvecoeur had, that the frontier was the very matrix of equality, but that it was a setting for degeneration as well as for regeneration. Here all men who were white were indeed on a par, or thought they were; here your innkeeper was not obsequious: if you did not want to sit down and dine with him at his own table, then you could leave and be damned! Here there were no servants, except black (and not many of those once you got beyond the tidewater); here workmen would work when it pleased them. Here the poor, if industrious, could win a competence in a decade and, if shrewd, a fortune in two.

All America was a melting pot—the phrase is Crèvecoeur's—but this was especially true on the frontier. Once past the tidewater, Louis-Philippe found Germans, Scots, Irish, and Swiss, all intermingled in the frontier towns, and living peaceably with each other. He saw, too, something no one could take for granted anywhere in Europe—religious toleration and equality. Presbyterians, Baptists, Lutherans, Anglicans, even a few Catholics, lived and worked—and fought—side by side without animosity and, what is more, they intermarried without so much as a by-your-leave. Here, too, he saw the beginnings of that cultural chauvinism which was for so long to mark the American mind—a chauvinism which assumed the superiority of everything American, and the corruption and decadence of everything European. And no wonder, what with the elementary fact that most Americans were here because they or their forebears had repudiated Europe; no wonder, what with the Revolution still in the consciousness of men, what with the spectacle of the French Revolution and the reaction to it before their eyes, what with Spain and

France and England stirring up trouble among the western Indians. Oddly enough, the royal princes did not encounter much of this hostility themselves, probably because they were clearly poor, because they accepted—with what grace they could muster—the hardships of frontier life, and because they were genuinely thankful to be in America rather than in some dungeon in France, or on the run in Europe.

Here, too, Louis-Philippe found that response to environment which was to be so characteristic of the whole of American history: the sheer physical response in height and weight of the men, in the survival of children and the longevity of adults; the cultural adaptation in adjusting institutions to new circumstances; the economic impact of general well-being and, with it, general social equality. Here he saw the operation of that instinct of voluntarism which was to strike de Tocqueville as perhaps the most important of democratic qualities: the readiness of men and women to band together to do whatever needed to be done—to hew out paths, to build stockades, to set up churches and schools, to govern themselves, with or without outside authority. Curiously enough, there was little of this initiative in matters that concerned only the amenities: food, drink, domestic comforts, the lubricant of good manners. Thus Louis-Philippe paints a hilarious picture of a night with the amiable Captain Chapman, on the lower Tennessee, with the four travelers bedded down (on the floor) in the one bedroom available, the captain and his wife sleeping quietly in one bed, their daughter and her young man occupying the other, and doing what came naturally to them. "Now what do you think of, *à la* those romances of Crèvecoeur and Brissot?" Louis-Philippe asked. And as for manners, he tells us that the Cherokees were more courteous and more hospitable than the white invaders.

It was the Indians, indeed, who fascinated Louis-Philippe, as they had fascinated Crèvecoeur and Volney and Chateaubriand, who devoted three of his romances to them. This was part of that romantic view of the New World and especially of Nature and the Indians, more widespread in Europe than in the United States. Montpensier's paintings are irretrievably romantic—what a passion he had for cascades and waterfalls and primitive forests—and Louis-Philippe, too, as it turned out, belonged very much in the romantic era. Here were, after all, so many of the quintessential elements of romanticism: distance, vastness, mountains and rivers and lakes that combined the sublime and the beautiful, the primitive—in Nature, in native races, and in the Negroes, pastoral virtue and innocence, simplicity, the childhood of man recreated.

The diary ends at Bardstown, in Kentucky. There was far more adventure ahead of the royal travelers than they had yet encountered: a journey to the Great Lakes and Niagara Falls, to the Genesee Valley, a canoe trip down the Susquehanna to Wilkes-Barre, and then a return to Philadelphia and a restoration, there, to the pleasures and excitements of society. The prince dined with Talleyrand and Alexander Hamilton in New York; he visited Boston, where he was entertained by stout Federalists like Harrison Gray Otis and Timothy Pickering. There he got word that his mother had been exiled to Spain, and the three young men embarked on a kind of nightmare return which landed them not in Spain but in Cuba, in Halifax, in New York for a second time, and eventually in England.

We need not follow the fortunes of Louis-Philippe beyond America. After a quiet decade in England he married the daughter of King Ferdinand of Naples; with the Bourbon restoration, he got back most of his estates and found himself a rich man. He lived quietly enough in Sicily. In 1830, Charles X was ousted as King of France, and—with the aged Lafayette presiding—Louis-Philippe was called to that throne to which he had long aspired. Perhaps he had learned something from his American trip: he called himself King of the French; he flew the tricolor, not the fleur-de-lis; he lived quietly, unostentatiously, dressed in business suits and carried—it was perhaps an English habit—an umbrella. When, in 1830, President Jackson revived the "French Spoliation Claims" for some twelve million dollars, King Louis-Philippe intervened to bring about an amicable settlement. Perhaps that gesture was inspired by affection for the country that had received him so hospitably when he was on the run.

Henry Steele Commager

Translator's Note

Louis-Philippe was king of France from 1830 to 1848. He was of the Orleans branch of the Bourbons, a direct descendant of Louis XIII through that monarch's younger son Philippe. Louis-Philippe was entitled Duc de Valois at birth, Duc de Chartres in 1785, and Duc d'Orléans at his father's death in 1793. He became king not in the normal course of events, but because France detested the reactionary Charles X, and Louis-Philippe was steady, moderate, legitimately if not directly in the royal line, and liked by a bourgeoisifying France for his adventurous (at one period even revolutionary) youth and his liberal view of monarchy.

Born in 1773, he traveled in the United States during 1796 and 1797. His often flavorful spelling of proper names has been preserved. Also his pleasantly inconsistent use of numerals and spelled-out numbers. Italicized words were either emphasized by him in the French or written originally in English.

Louis-Philippe's own notes are marked at the bottom of the page with an asterisk, the annotator's notes are numbered, and the translator's notes are marked with a dagger or set in brackets.

Stephen Becker

Map of Travels of the Princes of Orléans (1796–99)

The travels of the Duc d'Orléans and his brothers to the United States (1796–1799), after the map drawn up by the Musée de l'Histoire de France for the exhibition "Louis-Philippe" (Archives Nationales, 1974–1975). The journal of the trip only covers part of the first voyage, from March 25 to May 21, 1791.

•••••••••• Journey to Philadelphia–Nashville–Buffalo

–·–·–·–·– Journey to Maine

– – – – – Departure for New Orleans

Map labels:

MAINE · Portland · Portsmouth · Boston · Providence · 25 December 1799 · GREAT BRITAIN · 24 October 1796 · Hamburg · 21 September 1796 · Oct.–Dec. 1797 · New York · Philadelphia · Baltimore · Washington · Elmira · Carlisle · 10 December 1797 · Buffalo · Erie · Pittsburgh · Staunton · Charleston · Abingdon · NORTH CAROLINA · Niagara Falls · OHIO · INDIANA · ILLINOIS · Zanesville · Maysville · Lexington · Knoxville · GEORGIA · Louisville · Nashville · 10 May 1791 · Ohio R. · MISSOURI · Fort Jefferson · ALABAMA · MISSISSIPPI · LOUISIANA · 12 February 1798 · Natchez · New Orleans · Baton Rouge · Mississippi R. · Atlantic Ocean

Diary of My Travels in America

Begun 25 March 1797

A presumed portrait of Louis-Philippe
about 1795. Charcoal drawing
(collection of the Comte de Paris).
SERVICE PHOTOGRAPHIQUE DES
ARCHIVES NATIONALES.

We left Philadelphia before noon today, the three of us and Beaudoin, all on horseback. Our horses cost us $930 and our tack $70. Our luggage consists of four saddlebags and a like number of cloth coats and oilskin cloaks.

We took the road to Baltimore, by way of Wilmington and Havre de Grace. We dined in Derby and slept in Marcus-Hook,[1] just where I was united with my brothers. In general the countryside is pleasant. It is cleared forest land, obviously; except for an occasional small marsh, whatever is not *field* is *forest*. The real difference, to my eye, between this country and Europe is that the fields here are always enclosed by forests. Another difference, even more striking, is the height of the trees in those forests; almost all the woods here are of full-grown timber.

The 26th. We spent the second day of our journey in Wilmington, a small town nicely situated between Brandy-Wine and Christina-Creek. There are handsome houses here already, and the town is thriving. Its principal business is warehousing for Philadelphia. There are many Quakers. Just outside town is a poorhouse, a fairly large building for a region where large buildings hardly exist. In Wilmington, as in all American towns, I believe, the streets are laid out perfectly straight and intersect at right angles. Likewise the

[1] The Delaware River had frozen solid that winter, and the three brothers' reunion took place at Marcus Hook. Montpensier and Beaujolais found their elder brother quite changed.

Delaware River Front, Philadelphia.
Watercolor by Thomas Birch.
M. and M. Karolik Collection.

houses are uniformly built of brick in the same style as Philadelphia's.

Beyond Wilmington we proceeded through eight miles of scenic,
well-cultivated country as far as Christina, five miles from Newport,

where we dined. Some sandy yet marshy terrain begins there, with dwellings few and far between. From Christina to Elkton, which is to say over a stretch of eleven miles, there is no inn to be found. We slept at Mrs Boyd's place in Elkton. A good inn. Elkton is a small town surrounded by marshes and stagnant water, which did not deter mine host from insisting that it was a very healthy spot, and that only on the hillsides opposite were residents exposed to fever and disease. Leaving Elkton we rode to Charleston, a little village but one of the oldest settlements in Maryland. The Chesapeak lay before it like a beautiful lake.

The 27th. Toward noon we reached the Susquehanna ferry, across from Havre de Grace. The wind was so fierce that they refused to take us across, and passengers on the public coach were made to wait until quite late in the evening. We slept in the inn there, which was fair.

We stopped for a look at Cecil Furnace, below a waterfall on Cecil Creek of which Montpensier made a sketch. They cast cannon here for the American government. Not much of a place.

The 28th. After considerable trouble the four of us and our mounts boarded a single boat. One of the horses fell into the water, and we had the devil's own time hauling him back aboard. With a strong headwind we were forced to come about three times before we could land, and it was all the more vexatious because with a low boom swinging, each change of tack terrified our horses, and it was not easy to keep them calm.

Havre de Grace is only a very small place. They say that a company has just been organized to make a great city of it, with plans to put up thirty houses for a start. That may be, but meanwhile the place is next to nothing. All the Susquehanna's trade is at present shared between Philadelphia and Baltimore. But Havre de Grace will probably expand when they complete the recently begun canal to bypass the falls of the Susquehanna. In Baltimore someone told me that the port here was no good, and that the bottom was silting up; but as Baltimore may justly be suspected of commercial jealousy, the observation would have to be confirmed.

After crossing the Susquehanna we found the countryside richer: better cultivated, and the inhabitants seemingly more prosperous. We never reached Baltimore that day, having forgotten an oilskin cloak at our stop for dinner, and so we reined up at the Red Lion to send a messenger back for it.

The 29th. We reached Baltimore at one o'clock and took lodgings with the Evanses at "The Indian Queen." Before riding down into Baltimore one is treated to a panorama of the whole city, the port, and the bay, all of which together compose a splendid view. My brothers tell me that it looks much like Marseilles. The city seems quite large but comprises only 20,000 inhabitants. Market Street, the main avenue, is broad and handsome. The houses that line it are quite plain but brand new, for the city has been built up only recently; that is, it has achieved its present prosperity only in the last few years, for the town itself is quite old; but it seems that it owes its expansion

A waterfall in America, perhaps Cecil Creek, above the Susquehanna, which the princes visited 27 March 1797. Gouache, probably by Montpensier (collection of the Comte de Paris). PHOTO, FLAMMARION.

to the export of flour from the west. As it lies farther west than Philadelphia, Baltimore has found it possible to buy up western flour cheaper and consequently in greater quantity. Baltimore is trying to facilitate transportation and communication by increasing traffic along the Susquehanna. For its part, Philadelphia is making every effort to cut canals through, but they will not be worth the trouble if they are no better built than the one along the Schuylkill.[2]

We received many courtesies in Baltimore,[3] and dined at the homes of Messieurs Caton and Gilmore, and General Smith. We left on 2 April at 11 o'clock.

The 2d. The blacks of Maryland are slaves forever, they and their posterity. They have, nevertheless, according to what I was told in Baltimore, some advantages over those of Virginia and the southern states. They have the right (which the others have not) to present petitions to duly constituted authorities for emancipation, in certain cases. As a black or mulatto child always belongs to its mother's owner, it has been decided in this state that any man descended from

[2] In 1777 the Schuylkill was the scene of much fighting. At the time of the American defeat at Brandywine most of the British forces were camped along the river, on banks still famous for their beauty.

[3] They were made very welcome in Baltimore, and dined in particular with Robert Gilmore, an associate of the banker Willing. They made a number of purchases to round out their equipment: pistols, sabres, powder, pipes, pouches, and flints, which cost them $40. To smooth their way, Gilmore wrote out the text of a letter of credit in his own hand on the flyleaf of the Duc d'Orléans' travel notebook: "Should M. d'Orléans have occasion for funds during his journey, he will apply to Mr Burton at Richmond or Mr Nicholas at Lexington, who will furnish for the bills on [signed] Robert Gilmore et Co."

Antoine-Philippe, Duc de Montpensier,
younger brother of Louis-Philippe,
about 1791–1792. Painting by Charles
le Peintre (collection of the Comte de
Paris). PHOTO, CLICHÉ X.

a white woman has an inalienable right to recover his freedom if he can prove that fact.

The region between Baltimore and Bladensbourg, where we slept, is neither picturesque nor well farmed. We dined after 27 miles in a rather awful isolated inn belonging to Colonel Van Horn. We slept nine miles farther along, at Bladensbourg. A good inn.

On the 3d at 11 o'clock we reached Washington, or the federal city. The heat was oppressive and all the worse because the trees were not yet in leaf. The thorns and haws had barely begun to bud. Peach trees were in flower; one sees them growing wild here, though not in great numbers. It was a strange contrast, to see nature looking like January, and to be overwhelmed by a heat that we are more used to in the month of July.

The capital city is superbly situated. It is to lie on the banks of the Potowmack between the eastern and northwestern branches. Beyond the latter branch lies Georgetown, which is to be a suburb of the federal city one day. While awaiting that destiny Georgetown remains a rather pretty, rather crowded, rather commercial little town, and the capital itself consists only of a few scattered houses, with streets cut through the woods. Alexandria, on the Virginia bank of the Potowmack, is still larger than Georgetown, and like it, is destined to become a suburb of Washington, being included in the territory ceded by Virginia and Maryland to the nation. This district is a square ten miles on a side enclosing that stretch of the Potowmack on which the city is to be established.

On the highest ground, approximately at the city's center, they are constructing a building called the Capitol, which will be the meetinghouse of the two chambers of the federal government. This Capitol (of which I have seen the plans) is more specifically a peristyle in the Corinthian mode, or rather a rotunda flanked by two wings, of which the left is to be the House of Representatives and the right, the Senate. The latter, as well as the dome, is still at ground level, but the left wing will shortly be finished. Outside the Capitol a garden is to be planted on the slope dropping toward the Potowmack. To the right of the far end of this garden, and set some distance back, the President's residence rises; it is almost finished, and I fear that its architecture will appear heavy when the scaffolding is removed. The front entrance seems to me ridiculously small. Whatever their quality, these two large, complex edifices are the best looking, and even, I believe, the only such in the United States. Their façades are of stone. These stones are quarried from the Potowmack, and are faintly bluish. The construction of these buildings is an enormous expense, and a stonemason alone costs two dollars a day. The cost is estimated at a million dollars, and it is my impression that the result will not be much more beautiful than the pavilions at the new gates of Paris. Plans for the capital city were drawn up by a Frenchman (M. Lenfant).[4] The streets are cut through the woods or laid out among the orchards. They are named after the various states. The terrain is gently rolling.

The port formed by the eastern branch is very fine, but this port is, according to some, three miles, and according to others four, from Georgetown. Only one businessman is so far settled there (Mr Pary). His house is charmingly situated. While we were there he admitted one vessel, which he had chartered to carry a cargo of porcelain he'd had fired in Washington to Porto-Rico.

[4]Pierre L'Enfant (1754–1825), a military engineer who was inspired by the rebel cause, brought his talents to the American army in 1783. After architectural projects for the City

Mr Thomas Law,[5] brother of the lawyer who defended Mr Hastings,† has settled near the eastern branch. We had a letter from Mr Bingham[6] for him, and we lodged with him for a night. He complained at length about the Georgetowners' jealousy of the capital city, and their hindrance of his expansion by their efforts to attract settlers to their own neighborhood. Another reason Mr Law gave me for the scattered population is that people do not want to build in communities; they prefer isolation, and each builds on his own property to increase its value. If everything already built had been more concentrated, the capital city would by now be quite something, but as matters stand it is nothing.

Near the Potowmack Messieurs Morris and Nicholson[7] have built

---

of New York, he laid out plans for the new capital, whose construction along the Potomac had been decided in 1790.

[5]Thomas Law, who accompanied Talleyrand on his voyage in September 1794, had made a fortune in India, and marriage to a begum had further enriched him. Later still he married Washington's granddaughter. He was the brother of Edward Law, Baron Ellenborough (1750–1818).

†Warren Hastings (1732–1818) was the first Governor General of British India, when the functions and influence of the British East India Company were being assumed by the Crown and Parliament. For years he was accused of peculations and abuse of power. He resigned in 1785, but was nevertheless impeached in 1786. His trial began in 1788; he was acquitted in 1795.

[6]William Bingham (1752–1804) was a rich Philadelphia businessman who had married Thomas Willing's daughter; with Willing he had founded the first bank in the United States. He had lived in Europe for two years. His home was the most sumptuous in Philadelphia, and there he received numerous émigrés and travelers.

[7]Robert Morris (1734–1806), a friend and perhaps relative of Gouverneur Morris, together with John Nicholson, another Philadelphia businessman, had bought lands on the Susquehanna in Pennsylvania, on which the French settlement Asylum was built as a haven

a group of very beautiful houses which rumor has it cost $200,000. Some distance away is a large house without doors or windows on which the word *Hotel* is already painted in bold letters, and of a certainty there is none half so handsome in Philadelphia.

The disagreements and dissensions have considerably slowed the progress of the capital. Another reason, no less important, is the speculation and knavery of which it has been the object, to an extent that no buyer can be sure of his purchase, as the seller's title to the property is always dubious.

At any rate the principal reasons for the founding of Washington are first, the reciprocal jealousy of the large cities over the seat of government, and second, the desire to attract western trade to the east coast and divert it from the Gulf coast. Congress's purpose in founding Washington was to establish a metropolis for the west, and to substitute the Potowmack for the Mississippi. They say here that upstream the river is not navigable. I am not sure of that, but it may be that only such an obstacle could justify this project: the Ohio and the Potowmack are to be connected by a canal running from the latter into the Cheat River and the Monongahely.

Georgetown and Alexandria owe their expansion primarily to commerce with the west, and if Ohio River traffic can be routed as these people wish, I think Washington will become incontestably one of the biggest cities in North America.

for the royal family had they been able to escape from France. Morris was superintendent of finance [under the Articles of Confederation] but later went bankrupt in building speculation in Washington, and was imprisoned for debt from 1798 to 1801 in Philadelphia.

The site of Federal City originally belonged to Mr Caroll* and Mr Young. They deeded half their property to the nation in return for the enormous rise in value of the rest.

The 4th April, Mr Law escorted us to the office of the commissioners in charge of construction in Washington, and there we saw plans for the new buildings. He escorted us thence to Georgetown, separated from Washington only by the northwest branch. That is crossed by a new bridge, elegantly constructed. Georgetown is a pretty town built like an amphitheater on the left bank of the Potowmack. Just off Georgetown is an island of about eighty acres. They call it *Mason's island* after the Colonel Mason[8] who owns it all. The scarcity of mosquitoes along the Potowmack must make it all the more pleasant as a home. Above Georgetown there is a Catholic school established in a notably large building for this area. The riverbed narrows at Georgetown, the bluffs along its bank draw together and rise steeply,

---

*This Mr Caroll is not the former senator.

[8]Colonel Mason was exceedingly kind to the travelers. He was a friend of Etienne Cathalan, American consul in Marseilles, who with General Willot supervised the liberation of the Duc de Montpensier and the Comte de Beaujolais. Cathalan had refused reimbursement of their passage money and had even provided them with very useful supplies for the crossing. The young princes lived at his home after their release from Fort Saint-Jean, during the five or six days preceding their embarkation. The Comte de Beaujolais thanked Cathalan, in a letter addressed to him at Philadelphia, 13 August 1797, for having put them in touch (doubtless by a letter of introduction) with Colonel Mason: "In Georgetown in Maryland we saw Mr Mason who was extremely courteous to us. He spoke often of Mme Cathalan and yourself. With him we revisited the *falls* of the Potomac. He is widely known here as a friend to the French."

*Louis-Charles, Comte de Beaujolais,
youngest brother of Louis-Philippe,
about 1791–1792. Painting by Charles
le Peintre (collection of the Comte
de Paris).* PHOTO, CLICHÉ X.

and nature shows its wild side. Mr Law led us by a new road, not even finished, to where they have just built a bridge across the Potowmack, some four miles above Georgetown. The new road hugs the Potowmack valley. They took advantage of a very narrow stretch of riverbed to fling up a single-arched wooden bridge. Though not very wide, it is sturdy, constructed like Ulrich Grubenman's[9] in Switzerland. The suddenness of freshets on the Potowmack, with the water level occasionally rising thirty feet in one night along this stretch, compelled the builders to set the span very high. The major abutments are on the Virginia side and seem solidly constructed. This will no doubt be a successful project if the dike or jetty intended to connect it to the Maryland heights is built so as to allow sufficient outlet for ice during the spring breakup, and for water during the floods that often inundate the valley.

This bridge is located a bit below the *Little-Falls* at the mouth of Pimel Creek, which are aptly named and scarcely worth comment. We saw the canal that bypasses them. There is a double lock at one end. It is completely finished and on the Maryland side.

Mr Law leaving us at that spot, we proceeded alone, after passing the bridge, on the road to the great cataracts (*big* or *great falls*) on the Virginia side. They are a good ten miles farther. We had hoped to find an inn nearby, but were disappointed in our expectations. The inn had closed down two days before, and if not for the kindness of Colonel Mason, who was there by a lucky chance overseeing work on the canal (of which he is in charge), we should have been obliged to return, we and our horses both, without food or drink. He was so obliging as to supply the deficiency by persuading a local woman to give us dinner and to feed and water our horses.

[9]The Duc d'Orléans, who had resided in Reichenau in 1793–94 and been a professor at the college there, had admired its bridge, the work of Ulrich Grubenman, a celebrated Swiss architect who, with his brother Jean, had devised new methods of construction.

The first part of the canal is finished; it leads from the river to a sizable basin and is on a level with the upper stretch of the river. After the basin begins another channel, of which the larger part will be hewn out of rock. There will be six locks in this section. The last three will be very close together. There are several outlets to facilitate runoff during freshets and spates. This canal is dug on the Virginia side. The difference in level from highest point to lowest is 82 feet. They have allowed for 86 as a margin of safety. So subtracting no more than 7 feet from that height for the half-submerged rocks above and the swift current below, there would remain 75 feet for the height of the falls. That is less than the waterfall on the Rhine at Lauffen, which drops, I believe, 80 of our feet. Furthermore, the volume of water is considerably less, the roar is feebler, and Lauffen's charming landscape is here replaced by barren boulders. By a striking accident, some of those boulders form a natural dike that runs out into the river from the Maryland side, almost directly beneath the falls, sends some of the heavy flow swirling back, and channels it into a very narrow strait. However inferior this cataract may be to Lauffen's, here they claim that after Niagara it is the most beautiful in North America (*no, it is not*).

As there was not a single inn the whole way, in the evening we were obliged to return to Georgetown, where we arrived quite late. Colonel Mason came back with us.

*

*

*

30

The 5th April we had planned to leave in the morning and reach General Washington's home at Mount Vernon[10] in time for dinner, but because some laundry we had sent out was not yet ready, we were compelled to dine in Georgetown, and we were not able to set out until half past four. We crossed on the ferry at Georgetown and arrived at Mount Vernon at half past six, when the general welcomed us with great courtesy. His house is splendidly situated beside the Potowmack, fifteen miles below the city named after him. Though the house is of wood,* it looks well, and before it lies what might be a playground carpeted in green. The general owns ten thousand acres of land around Mount Vernon. Hardly half of it is under cultivation. There are about 400 blacks scattered among the different farms. These unfortunates reproduce freely and their number is increasing. I have been thinking that to accomplish their emancipation gradually and without upheaval it might be possible to grant them first a status in mortmain by depriving their owners of the right to sell them. Virginia law imposes the same punishment on a master who kills a slave as on any other murderer, but the law is very rarely applied; as slaves are denied by statute the right to bear witness, the charge is never proved. General Washington has forbidden the use of the whip

---

[10]The death of his half-brother Lawrence had made Washington a very rich Virginia land-owner. He lived at Mount Vernon, his country house on the Potomac, when he was not in public service.

*Mount Vernon was given to the general by his brother, out of respect for whom the general kept the wooden house. His brother served in the Royal Navy under Admiral Vernon at Cartagena [in 1740. Mount Vernon was named for the admiral].

on his blacks, but unfortunately his example has been little emulated. Here Negroes are not considered human beings. When they meet a white man, they greet him from a distance and with a low bow, and they often seem amazed that we return their greeting, for no one here does so. All agricultural labor in Virginia is performed by blacks, who on the various farms are housed in wretched wooden shacks here called *quarters*. Usually these shacks swarm with pickaninnies in rags that our own beggars would scorn to wear. So why should we be surprised if the blacks are lazy, when their labor never profits them? On the contrary, it profits those whom they must naturally hate.

The last census in Virginia showed 770,000 inhabitants. It is estimated that some three-fourths of them are blacks. This ratio is terrifying, and will sooner or later prove deadly to the southern states. Ideas of freedom have already made headway among them; apparently Quakers, Anabaptists, and Methodists circulate the doctrine. The general's blacks told Beaudoin that they had clubs in Alexandria and Georgetown, that Quakers came to visit, and that they hoped they would no longer be slaves in ten years—not that they wanted to follow the example of the blacks in Santo-Domingo, they would do no harm to any man, etc. . . . The general's cook ran away, being now in Philadelphia, and left a little daughter of six at Mount Vernon. Beaudoin ventured that the little girl must be deeply upset that she would never see her father again; she answered, *Oh! sir, I am very glad, because he is free now.* The general's house servants are mulattoes, some of whom have kinky hair still but skins as light as ours. I noticed one small boy whose hair and skin were so like our

The Little Falls of the Potomac, visited by the princes 4 April 1797. Gouache, attributed to Montpensier (collection of the Comte de Paris). PHOTO, FLAMMARION.

own that if I had not been told, I should never have suspected his ancestry. He is nevertheless a slave for the rest of his life.

We left Mount Vernon the 9th. The general was kind enough to give us letters, and some comments in his own hand on our proposed itinerary. Messieurs de La Fayette and Frestel[11] escorted us as far as Alexandria, where we dined together.

We took the wrong road out of Alexandria, heading for Newgate instead of Leesburg. We found a transverse road and cut across, arriving late, and in wretched weather, at a detestable inn called *The Old Court House*, because local courts once convened there.

The 10th. We crossed a region almost uninhabited, and consequently covered with vast forests. The land seemed poor and the roads were awful. True, recent rains had played havoc with them. The sandy composition of the soil helped them dry quickly. For some time we enjoyed views of the mountain called *Shugarloaf*. It is in Maryland, some way from the Potowmack, the tallest I have yet seen in America.

In Leesburg we dined at Robert's, where we found the Colonel Ball for whom the general had given us a letter.† I presented it to him; his lively insistence that we lodge with him three miles from there was irresistible, and the only dispensation granted us was an exemp-

---

[11]George-Washington de La Fayette (1779–1840), son of the French general, had lived in the United States since 1795. First he went to live with La Colombe, his father's former aide-de-camp; then he traveled with his tutor Frestel.

†Surely a cousin. Washington's mother was a Ball.

tion from Colonel Thomas Lee's dinner invitation the next day. Generally in such a dull region the only reward of visits and dinners is boredom and a useless protraction of the journey. What really interests me is the temper of the country, the state of its agriculture, dwellings, population, etc.*

Colonel Ball has a lovely property comprising 1,500 acres along the Potowmack. He calls this estate *The Big Springs*. It is a handsome holding that anyone would envy if it were not in Negro country. There is still no house but the one he found there, little more than a shack. Nevertheless he offered us a room with *two* good beds, which pleased us mightily. As we entered the house he did something that might have astonished me in another country: he held out his arm so I could help him out of his redingote. I thought of my own frequent pleas for help in putting mine *on*, and did not hesitate to take him by the sleeve. This won me no no thanks, as he carried off the redingote without a word to me.

The 11th. We rode through hilly, picturesque country in the foothills of the Montagnes Bleues *(blue ridge)*, which run from southwest to northeast and are the first range in from the coast. They are not high. There is little or no bare rock to be seen. The slope is not precipitous, and the forest** stretches uninterruptedly to the summits, which are

---

*Passed through Waterford, a Quaker town. No slaves at all. Very few in this area.
**Almost all oak, mixed with a few pines.

more like hilltops. Moreover, the range is drawn up like a regiment, and the eye follows its undeviating spine irresistibly.

We halted at a cabin (an old *log-house* called *Biard's Tavern* after the proprietor) in a gorge called *Keyes's gap*. We were in a miserable wooden shanty, but Biard is having a house built that will be finished by fall. He is a Pennsylvanian, like his wife. They settled here 24 years ago, cleared the land, and own a hundred acres.

The view from the far slopes of the Blue Ridge Mountains would be very beautiful if only the trees did not obscure it. The Shenando or Shenandoah flows at the foot of the range, between it and the quite distant mountains to the north. We crossed the Shenando at *Keyes's ferry*[12] at the foot of the range. The banks of the river are charming, and this whole region looks like Switzerland. At Keyes's ferry we left the main road and detoured to Harper's ferry, to see where the confluence of the Potowmack and the Shenando cuts a gap in the blue range. The scene is quite wild, and much like the banks of the Rhine in the Grisons near Ratrüns, but that resemblance seemed the only remarkable thing about it. I have seen a score of places in Switzerland where rushing waters have carved out infinitely more striking gaps, not to mention the amazing irruption of the Rhine into the Via Mala. Above the confluence of the two rivers there are rapids, passable by a canal on the Maryland side. There is another a few miles upstream on the same side. According to the maps this great gap is the only

---

[12]The ferries, which were sailboats or flat-bottomed rowing boats, sometimes gave their names to the river—or estuary—crossing they served.

one in the whole blue range. Furthermore there are few large rock faces and those not very steep. We were there at sunset, and the scene did not strike me as very remarkable. The inn is on the Virginia side. We returned to sleep at Charlestown that same night. Beautiful countryside and the beginnings of good agriculture.

The two inns were full because of a college ceremony followed by a ball. We spent a very bad night in the billiard room. Charlestown, in Berkley county, is a small city of about 100 houses, according to the local folk.

The 12th. We came to Winchester for dinner. The countryside monotonous and indifferently farmed. They are still clearing, and there is certainly plenty still to be done. There are many Germans in the town and its environs. We lodge with Busch, who is from Manheim. He keeps a good inn. The town is fair-sized. There is a Catholic church for the Germans, most of whom came from the banks of the Rhine by way of Holland. The weather was hot and oppressive all day.

We spent the entire afternoon of the 12th in Winchester. We were even planning to dine there the 13th, because the laundry we wanted done could not be ready sooner, but insolence on the part of our host resolved us to leave without dining. He flew into a fury over our simple query to his black, whether we might not dine in privacy; and he marched into the room in a rage, shouting that no such request had ever been made before in his establishment, that not even General Washington would dare make it, and that he would absolutely not stand for two dinner tables in his house. We replied that he was the master of the house, that we had not dreamed so simple a question could trigger so much impertinence, and that since he took that tone we declined to dine at all on his premises and would depart instanter, which we did, after settling our score for 13 dollars. That scene prevented delivery of the letter for Winchester kindly given us by the general. It must also be admitted that we felt no great desire to prolong our stay.

The 13th we arrived at Newtown for dinner and spent the night at Strasburg, which the Americans call Stoward's town. As we approached Strasburg the countryside seemed very pleasant, but we suffered a thunderstorm accompanied by the most violent rainfall I can remember. It was so fierce that our horses could not endure it by the flank, and finally turned their hindquarters to the blast.

Strasburg is what they call a city here, but in Europe it would be just a small village. It is in a lovely region. It was founded by Germans, and entering the inn I felt myself wafted to Germany, in the presence of so much of its custom and contrivance. We managed a good supper in the room of the host and hostess, where there was a stove, and benches in an alcove. We had two good adjoining rooms and four beds. Most of the Germans here are from the Palatinate and the banks of the Rhine. They traveled downstream to Holland, whence they were shipped off to America. The hostess is a Pennsylvanian like almost all the Germans hereabouts. They speak a corrupt German something like Swabian. Beer is available in these Germans' homes, and theirs are the only inns where we have been able to buy it. Ordinarily all you find here is rum or whiskey, Port or Madeira, and porter.

Strasburg is situated between the northern mountains and an intermediate chain between them and the Blue Ridge Mountains. The Shenando flows between that intermediate range and the northern mountains, and is joined, a few miles below Strasburg, by a river flowing out of the southern valley, called simply *South river*. These names *South river, North river,* etc. . . . are so common in America that great confusion arises. This confusion is not limited to that one example; when the country is more densely populated and its cities are no longer villages, people will realize how awkward is this constant repetition of cities' and counties' names, and no geography will prove more difficult to master than the American. But back to my mountains.† I have never been able to learn the name of that intermediate chain and to tell the truth I do not believe it has one. It rises at Strasburg above the mouth of the South River, and its shape there has earned it the name *Three tops mountain;* a bit farther along *Short Ass,* etc. It is about fifty miles long.

The 14th. The country became more and more mountainous, the pines grew denser and were finally the only kind of tree in the valley. They grew in groves that ended in arrowheads on the mountainsides but never reached the peaks. The soil in these parts is arid and the only

42

---

† A gentle pun. "Je reviens à mes moutons" means "As I was saying" or "But I digress." Louis-Philippe writes, "Je reviens à mes montagnes."

local product is pine tar. We dined with Mr Golladey, whose grandfather was a French refugee. We are still in the pine forests, but after we drop down a way, the pines thin out and the terrain improves. We passed through New Market, five miles farther on, and after missing a German tavern in *Merz* or *March*, we slept at another German's, named *Freÿ*, in a squalid boozing-ken a mile down the

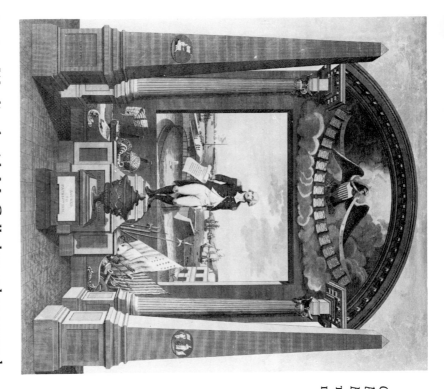

George Washington, 1798. Engraving by Cornelius Tiebout, after Charles Buxton. I. N. PHELPS STOKES COLLECTION, THE NEW YORK PUBLIC LIBRARY, ASTOR, LENOX AND TILDEN FOUNDATIONS.

road. He and his wife were Pennsylvanians; she neither spoke nor understood English.

The 15th. We took our noon meal at a little town called *Kized's town* twelve miles from Frey's. There is another road, to the right, from New Market to Staunton and a city called *Harrison'sburg,* capital of Rockingham county, about the same distance from *Kized's town. We* dined at Hudson's tavern and slept in Staunton at the General Washington Inn, proprietor *Peter Heiskell,* a Pennsylvania German. Excellent inn. Staunton's environs are quite hilly. The town consists of about 300 houses or families, for each family has its own. Bad weather during the day.

*The 16th.** The country still hilly. We begin to glimpse the northern mountains to our right. To our left rise others. Between the two ranges the land is varied, sometimes copses and groves, then smaller ranges cutting through the valleys, etc. We dined at David Steel's house halfway to Lexington. This poor unfortunate was captured by Parleton's† corps, and after he had surrendered they fetched him two blows of the saber to the head, so he says, bashing out a piece of bone that his wife showed us. M. de Chastellux stayed with them on his way to and from the Natural Bridge.[13] Steel told us funny stories. We

---

*Oaks on the southern slopes are greening.

†Probably a slip of the pen for Tarleton.

[13]The Duc d'Orléans was interested, but less impressed than other travelers of the time, by

reached Lexington late. It was full night and we had great trouble locating the ford across the north branch of the James river; we even missed it; we even missed the road; and we were a long time finding it and then crossing another stream that lay beyond. The town is only half a mile from it. Weather less bad than the day before. Put up at the Red Lion, proprietor Hanna; nice people, but a beggarly inn.

The 17th. Stopover in Lexington, [Virginia].

The 18th. One of our horses being lame, we did almost the whole day's journey on foot. Country still mountainous, indifferently farmed and uninteresting.* We made a halt at Captain Bartley's inn,

the Natural Bridge, called in Virginia "Rocky Bridge," which was considered a wonder of nature. Diagrams of it were drawn up by an engineering officer, the Baron de Turpin.

*No sight of the northern mountains, but only Shore Hill, etc.

A page from one of the two notebooks of the travel diary. PHOTO, SERVICE PHOTOGRAPHIQUE DES ARCHIVES NATIONALES.

a real hovel. The master of the house is a decent sort and a jokester. He guided us to the Natural Bridge, about a mile and a half from his inn. This is a very unusual bridge. It spans *Cedar creek*, a very small stream. It is a tall mass of rock which seems to have been hollowed out by the water's steady action, perhaps like the rifts of the Rhône; and as the mass of rock is quite narrow, it would seem that the earth above and below the bridge either collapsed or was swept away by the stream and left the bridge suspended between two masses of rock. Its height in the middle is 71 yards above the water. In that same spot the rocky arch is 50 feet thick. The gap at water level is 40 feet; above, the span is 30 yards. There is a path below the bridge by which one can stroll under the arch along the stream. This is truly an exceptional sight, and though the region is scrubby, the bridge is surely picturesque. Otherwise it seems to me that a good sketch and a precise description should do the trick, and that it is not really worth a second trip. Captain Bartley gave me all those measurements. Today was very cold; it froze last night and snowed this morning, but the snow did not stick.

The 19th. Almost all the oaks leafing, and consequently the forests turning green. Yet in this respect there is considerable variation among the oaks. Some are altogether green, others are only budding, and for still others it might be January. This does not seem to depend on the exposure, for we find many examples proving the contrary; more probably it is due to the greater or lesser warmth of the ground. The soil here is full of clay, mixed with more or less sand and good humus, and is consequently yellowish or reddish, never black like the rich soil of France. All the forests I have so far seen consist wholly of oaks and pines (in the mountains). Of course I except a scattering of other sorts.

In leaving Captain Bartley's we crossed Cedar creek, which drives a mill wheel. The closer we approached the James river, the sandier, and therefore less cultivated, the soil. We dined on the left bank of that river, at Padensburg, a town of twenty souls, as they themselves boast. Their inn is fairly good. We crossed the river by ferry. The district is rather picturesque. It stretches along the James river's course through the Blue Ridge Mountains.

The landscape improves beyond the river and there are more people. About four miles along, the road forks. One fork leads to *Fincastle*, also called *Botitourt*, also called *Munroe*, and crosses the *Kanhaway*, which along this stretch is called *New river*, at *Pepper's ferry*. That is the right-hand fork. The other passes through a new town called *Amsterdam* and crosses the Kanhaway at *English's ferry*. That is the better road. The two ferries have given their names to the two roads, *Pepper's road* and *English's road*. The latter is a bit longer, but better in all respects. We slept in Amsterdam at a good inn, proprietor Mr Botts, 15 miles from Padensburg and five from Fincastle, which is twelve miles from the river. There is a road from Fincastle to English's road.

In Botts's tavern we found ourselves among a large group of travellers much like those Fielding describes. They were headed for Kentucky and uneasy about the latest massacre by the Indians. In their anxiety they wanted us to swell their number, but we ignored the plea, knowing only too well the miseries such a crowd could cause in the region's tiny inns. Also, every man has his own way of traveling and travelers are mutually annoying; and aside from that, nothing is more boring than bored people who want to talk and have nothing to talk about. During the three hours they made us wait, as usual, for a few slices of fried ham and coffee with brown sugar, there were some who never shut up for a moment and others who never said a word but could not stop yawning, scratching, belching, etc.

The 20th. Instead of sallying forth at dawn, as they had boasted they would, our wayfarers only started out at 7 o'clock, leaving the staff at the inn less than overwhelmed by their generosity, and having managed several disagreements with their host.

We dined at the home of Mr Coles, a Pennsylvania German. The countryside unimpressive except here and there. Greenery thick, and in the oak forests whole groves are all green. We crossed the river Raunoake six times and went to sleep at Colonel Lewis's, two miles above Colonel Hancock. A pleasant and comfortable place. His house is charmingly set on a foothill of the Alleghanys and surrounded by lush meadows. In the old days there was a fort here (Voss's fort) that was captured by the Indians.

The 21st. Our road went on rising gently until we had reached the summit of the hills called the Alleghanys. I do not know their height above sea level; not great, I suspect, because they rise above the valley floors no higher than the hills around Paris, and the Blue Ridge

The U.S. warship America, aboard which Louis–Philippe made the crossing from Hamburg to Philadelphia, 24 September to 24 October 1796. Lithography from a painting by Theodore Gudin commissioned by Louis–Philippe. PHOTO, SERVICE PHOTOGRAPHIQUE DES ARCHIVES NATIONALES.

Mountains are real mountains by comparison. To look at the Alleghanys one would never think they are one of the watersheds of this immense continent. Our own continent, though much smaller, has mountains so much more majestic; which brings us to the notion that perhaps the effect attributed to the trade winds is real, that the cumulative level of the sea along these coasts is higher than ours, that these waters, ebbing more reluctantly, are deeper and more widespread than on our continent, and that this laggard drainage prevents them from leaching off the soil and vegetable matter that still carpet the Alleghanys as most likely they used to carpet the Alps.

The Alleghanys (in the region where I crossed them) are covered with oaks; one sees hardly any pines. The soil is dry and arid. It is no more than a stony sand, not cultivable. There are no great masses of rock to be seen, and if not for the river currents and even more the map, the traveler would never believe himself in one of the principal ranges of North America. They say that around Pittsburg the mountains are craggier and higher than around here; we shall see about that on the way back. Crossing the Alleghanys I saw evidence of the Americans' ignorance, or laziness, about mapping their roads. The one we followed crossed over the tallest of the rounded hills, leaving vales left and right where it would have been far easier to cut a road because with the land overgrown and no streams in the area, there would be no cliffs or swamps to hinder the work, just trees to fell, the same as on the crests. The only way I could make sense of this road was by assuming that the first travelers who blazed a trail across the Alleghanys were attracted to the highest ground by their impatience to see the land to the west, and that sheer laziness led the road builders to follow that trail and spare themselves the trouble of cutting a new one.

The western slope of these mountains struck us as infinitely worse than the eastern. The soil is sandy and dry, the land is flatter, and the springs rarer. The vegetation is much less varied and flourishing than on the other slope. Here, not an oak in bud, where we had before seen

whole forests greening; the haws and sloes have only just begun to green and are no further along than those in Maryland at the beginning of the month.

We halted at a tiny village of about ten houses called Christiansburg, the seat of Montgomery County. It is nine miles from Colonel Lewis's.

Before continuing I should like to mention the notable height of men and girls on this side of the Shenando Valley. It seems to be increasing still, for most of the young people seem taller than their elders.

The countryside was about the same as far as the valley of the Big Kanhaway, which around here they call *New river*. The settlements here are few and squalid. From all I heard, they exist only along the road. The Big Kanhaway valley is better, though sparsely settled. It seems that fear of the Indians infected this area until the peace of '94.[14] There is no inn at English's ferry. We dined two miles on the other side with some Irishmen who have given the name *New Dublin* to a shanty they've been living in for six years. We slept in the home of an old man named Carter who has just sold his house and his 700 acres for 400 pounds U.S.† and who is shutting down his inn tomorrow. He is moving a few miles farther along on the Kanhaway. For some twenty miles the road runs within four or five miles of that river.

[14]Doubtless the treaty that followed the battle of Fallen Timbers, won by General Anthony Wayne, who put an end to Indian resistance in the region.
†Sterling was still in use, along with dollars, as legal tender at the time.

The 22d. We halted at Fort Chiswel to have a horse shod. To the left of the road there was a big fort torn down since the peace. Before and beyond the fort you cross Read creek. The soil still indifferent, though better than what we saw as we emerged from the Alleghanys. We dined at Marshall's in Wythe, a village of ten or twelve houses, seat of the county of that name. A handsome house and a fine inn for the region. *Pepper's road* meets the other road here. After dinner we weathered a terrible storm, and we spent the night with a German named Kätternring.

The 23d. Still rotten weather and indifferent country, the soil being generally yellow and sandy as it was east of the Alleghanys. We ran into some emigrants from North Carolina on their way to Cumberland. They say that last year a prodigious number of emigrants left that state for the same settlement, which is already sizable. Kätternring was a Tory during the war. He was arrested and taken to Staunton, and they confiscated a mill built of stone that he had worked not far from his present home. He has only 200 acres of land left.

We had dinner at Atkins's, a good inn. His house is on the Holstein river.[15] That night we slept at Colonel Campbell's; we had met him the night before and he all but forced us to come home with him, assuring us that we would find no tolerable inn until five miles from Abingdon. He lives on the left bank of the Holstein river, in a setting

---

[15]The Holstein River, which, joining the Clinch and the French Broad, forms the Tennessee River, a tributary on the left bank of the Ohio.

"Louis-Philippe proclaimed king." Félix Auvray. Valenciennes: Musée des Beaux-Arts. PHOTO, SERVICE GIRAUDON.

that would be lovely if the land were cleared; but, although he has six sons and several Negroes, he settles for what he cleared when he first arrived. And yet he has 3,000 acres here. I do not know what he and his sons do all day, and because he seems a fine fellow I asked him point blank. He answered that because he owns property in other parts he is always on the go and never at home.

I saw sugar maples on his property and again enjoyed the sight of their huge branches bowing earthward. I have often used their sugar in my coffee, which sweetening seems to me every bit as good as the other. It is impossible to estimate the yield of this product because it varies with the weather and with the trees themselves. It seems that America's changeable climate is the most favorable for these trees, as the sap only flows at the end of December, when a warm day with a thaw follows a cold night. In this area are trees that yield up to 15 pounds of brown sugar. There are many such hereabouts. Wild grapevines are another American plant that must subtly alter our impression of the landscape and differentiate it from our own. They always grow about another tree, twining to its upper limbs, whence tendrils droop to the ground. They produce very tart grapes, edible only after a frost. Apparently their leaves unfold very late, for we saw only buds on the other slope of the Alleghanys, and on this side they are much as they were in January.

The colonel had us sleep in one room with two of his sons. Montpensier was assigned to be my wife and Beaujolais was reserved for the elder son of the house. He yearned to decline that honor, but resigned himself, to avoid giving offense. Beaudoin slept on the floor with another son. The colonel is a stout fellow. He thinks he knows all about French matters, and like all foreigners knows next to nothing. He asked me what had become of the *Duc de Chartres*. I replied that I believed I had once borne that name. This revelation stunned him, though he knew perfectly well who I was. It redoubled his courtesy and deference, and he told me that my serenity was incredible, and that if he had lost all that I have lost he would be heartbroken.

He had taken it into his head that his ancestors were natives of Normandy and had followed William the Conqueror to England. He claimed that they called themselves *Camille* then, later anglicized to *Camell* and then *Campbell*, from which he concluded that Camille Desmoulins,† whom he called Camille *Dessemoulines*, must be a relative. He was absolutely serious.

The 24th. We did not leave the colonel's until eleven o'clock, after waiting three hours for a terrible breakfast. He gave me seven letters to various friends, which for the most part were not the sort of letter one would pass along, but he meant everything well and we can only be grateful to him.

We dined 16 miles from his place; there was truly not a single tolerable inn before that one, which was itself, come to think of it,

---

†Camille Desmoulins (1760–94) was an antiroyalist French journalist and politician. His inflammatory speech of 12 July 1789 began the revolution in the streets that led to the capture of the Bastille two days later. He was an associate of Danton, and was executed during the Reign of Terror, as were many moderates.

intolerable. There is no good one except at Captain Green's* six miles from Abingdon. We lost our way by proceeding straight ahead instead of turning right. We reached Abingdon at nightfall, having covered 30 miles. There we stayed "Au Cheval noir," a poor sort of inn just opened by Baldwin. The good one burned down three days ago. There is a good one a mile farther along at Captain Craig's.** Rotten weather.

The 25th. We tarried in Abingdon to have two saddles repaired. I learned to my great surprise that the plot of land whereon we lodged, a half acre with four houses and stables, was worth 5,000 dollars. Abingdon boasts about 30 houses. The soil is rich and black. There are swamps that could be drained and would make fine meadows. We dined at Major Fulkinson's 12 miles from Abingdon. The countryside we passed through was one great forest with a few bogs and almost no houses. The major has a handsome property of 150 acres that he cleared himself. He has been settled there for 24 years. There is a copious spring near the house. He is 8 miles from the main branch of the Holstein river. There is a shorter road that starts at Captain Craig's. On a further 450 acres Fulkinson thinks he has a thousand sugar maples. This sugar is excellent. There are no others in this area, and they export very little. Everyone sees to his own supply. After dinner much forest again and few houses, though toward the end,

*That is not precisely the name.
**There is a fork. We to the right.

many more than just outside Abingdon. A few excellent springs. Good weather. All the trees leafing and many of them quite green, especially in their higher reaches.

We slept at the home of James Campbell, an Irishman who came into the region twenty-three years ago without a penny and now owns a fine house and extensive lands he himself cleared. We fared famously at his place. The house is situated between the two lines that the overlapping states of Virginia and North Carolina claim as their respective boundaries. He believes that in the end he will be declared a resident of Virginia; in the meantime he can vote in both states. The gap between the two lines is no more than two or three miles.

The 26th. The woods entrancing and in some stretches entirely green. The wild grapevine is one of the last to leaf. Seven miles from Campbell's there are two roads. One runs down to Ross's forge and then rejoins the road we left after Craig's. The other bears right and crosses the north branch of the Holstein river near the widow Wills's. They told us the latter was better and shorter. It is not bad, but apparently there are fewer inns than on the other road, where at least there is one good one at the forge 16 miles from Campbell's. On this road, however, Peter Morris turned us away, saying he had no provisions, and sent us along to the widow Wills. This widow told us the same story, and even buying oats for the horses was excessively troublesome. The widow Williams is two miles farther along, but her house being off the road, we missed it. We stopped at another house, and they sent us on again to Mr Smith's, where, they said, *We should get a good entertainment.* The *entertainment* consisted of what they call *hoacakes,* that is, a pastry made of cornmeal and water which they cook on an iron sheet called in English . . . .

We ate it with butter and milk and that was our dinner. And Mr Smith has only an old *log-house* where he sells whiskey (the liquor distilled from grain), which is still the region's favorite beverage. That night we reached Mr Armstrong's, where we had a good supper in the local fashion, having made 35 miles during the day.

We crossed the north branch of the Holstein river in a ferry. The boatman kept us waiting three-quarters of an hour. His delay was deliberate, so we commandeered his boat and were about to shove off when he hurried up, quite angry, and on the other side he tried to hold us to a ransom of *nine* pence instead of *six,* but we held firm and he got nothing for his insolence.

Tonight we saw five wild turkeys. They are black and white. The Negro at Mr Armstrong's, where we are spending the night, killed a buck this morning and they served it at supper. There is plenty of game in this area; we see many common gray grouse and sometimes even a red one. A bluish dove is very common, and there are forest magpies, or rather hoopoes with red heads, white bellies, and slate-gray wings and back. There are also winey-red cardinals and others completely scarlet. The birds hereabouts sing very little, which deepens the melancholy of the forests; but now that the trees are green, we hear more of them. The woods are quite beautiful. The oaks tower to an extraordinary height; some are enormous around the trunk. But however beautiful the forests, they do become monotonous. A landscape cannot be beautiful where there are only trees. Only a blend of meadows, tilled fields, and human dwellings composes a truly pleasant countryside that charms the eye. But here nature seems dead; the dwellings are so few and far between that the forest seems endless, and when we do reach the end it proves only a few cleared acres, where we have hardly time to glimpse the sun and be reassured that we are still in a land something like our own!

The indolence and churlishness of the workingmen around here are unparalleled. When a horse throws a shoe, you can cover twenty-five miles and call upon five or six farriers before you find one willing to work. If the least thing goes wrong with a saddle, or clothes, or a boot, you cannot find a soul to make repairs, and the other day a cobbler answered us, *"Yes, that's right, I'm a shoemaker, and sometimes I work, but I'm not in the mood right now."*

The food in the inns is nothing much; generally it amounts to no more than fried fatback and cornbread. Eggs have disappeared and the potatoes are finished. In the better places they make us little wheatcakes that are rather good. There is coffee everywhere, but bad, very weak. The sugar is always black muscovado, or unrefined maple sugar, which I like better. We had tea only once and it was good, but it is not to be found. Nowhere are there chamber pots; we asked for one at Mr J. Campbell's and were told that *there were broken panes in the windows.* The reply was perfect for a game of cross questions and crooked answers. There were indeed many broken panes, and it is a rare thing here to sleep in a hermetically sealed room. The other day, being in a loft, we were looking for the window or opening that should do service for a chamber pot. We found it 10 feet up, and so we insisted on some sort of receptacle; they brought us a kitchen kettle!

Most of the houses consist of one large room on the ground floor with two facing doors left open all day to cool it and air it, and an attic or loft where travelers sleep in pairs.

The 27th. We made a halt at *Rogersville*, also called *Hawkins Court House.* There are only four or five houses in the village. A little before you reach it, the road to the blacksmith's turns off. Mr John Mitchell keeps an inn along this road that will be very elegant when it is finished. There was no hay, and to supply the deficiency they turned our mounts out into a field of rye. We were compelled to make a halt there for various repairs. We slept fourteen miles farther along, at the home of Mr Joel Dyers, who is an honest and good-natured man but had no butter in the house. The day was very hot and we arrived late, and saw many will-o'-the-wisps. The countryside is not bad, though the landscape is monotonous. Mr Dyers claims that he has never once in his sixteen years here let his land lie fallow. Dwellings scattered; the land promising a fair prospect when finally cleared. Several times we rode beside the Holstein river, which winds constantly and whose banks are most pleasant.

The 28th. We made a halt at Colonel Or's place, a rather large house a mile above the fork of the Cumberland and Kentucky roads. It is

Louis-Philippe, King of France. During his reign, the king strolled the streets of Paris as freely as he had roamed the wilds of America. THE NEW YORK PUBLIC LIBRARY.

five miles from the Holstein river. Below the fork the land becomes unproductive. One crosses a district that produces little more than pines. We dined at Mr Bunch's, a miserable hovel. If it were only a hovel, that would be bearable, but the surliness, the peevish and grudging reception of travelers, I found most intolerable.[16] We slept at Mr Parkins'. On the last stretch of road the countryside was worse than ever. Stunted pines, much swamp, plenty of rough spots, and at night a tremendous roar of toads and frogs. The flies and insects are becoming oppressive. They say there are prodigious numbers of them in summer. Very hot.

The 29th. Still nasty, inhospitable country, sparsely settled. We reached Knoxville early. It would be quite picturesque if not for the wearying regularity of streets and houses in American towns. The Holstein river, which flows below the town, is broad and beautiful. We bathed in it; the day was very hot. Five years ago there was not a single house here. Now there are over a hundred. We are lodging in one of the oldest, but laziness has so pervaded the way of life that they have not yet plugged up the holes in the outer walls cut for scaffolding when they built the house. There are five of these openings in our room, and scarcely a whole pane in the windows. Our horses are indifferently cared for, but the common board (where we are obliged by local custom to take our meals) is not bad.

[16]The Marquis de Chastellux had already noted [in his travel diary] that most inns received travelers "with indifference," as "more trouble than they are worth." The innkeepers were often well-to-do farmers and even former officers, required by local law to keep public accommodation on certain roads. These way-stops often served also as currency exchanges. The food available was generally inadequate and occasionally execrable. Horses suffered even more than people. In the wooded stretches there was no forage to be found, but only grain, corn, or oats.

We left Knoxville toward two in the afternoon of April 29th. First we took a ferry across the Holstein, and then we halted for the night at Mary'sville. There are a few farms in this area that seem rather good. The immaturity of the fruit trees indicates that the orchards are not very long established.[17] Mary'sville is new, founded only fifteen months ago. It is the seat of Blount County and was named Mary'sville after Madame Blount.[18] Mary'sville is between *Little river* and the *Tennassee*. Their divergence will determine the frontier with the Cherokees. It may almost be assumed that Mary'sville will be on their side of the line. If that happens, this settlement is doomed; for by the terms of the latest treaty all dwellings erected by whites on Indian territory are to be evacuated one month after the boundaries are set. This demarcation is currently being carried out by three commissioners from the United States government and three Indian commissioners. And however unhappy those who lose their homes, there are some who should have expected it, because they settled these lands on their own initiative without anyone's permis-

[17] Like all travelers of his period, the Duc d'Orléans took great interest in agricultural methods different from those used in Europe. Later, in 1811, the sight of six superb banana trees beneath his window in Palermo inspired him to try transplanting tropical vegetation to Sicily. From England he ordered ipecacuanha seeds, a cinchona tree, and currant bushes, and he contemplated planting other varieties, like mahogany, breadfruit, arrowroot, and tapioca, as well as pineapple, a fruit unknown in Sicily. He saw possible prosperity in these plantings should he be compelled to remain in Sicily.

[18] It was no doubt the wife of Senator William Blount (1749–1800, Superintendent of Indian Affairs in Tennessee from 1790 to 1796) who gave her name to the town of Maryville.

sion or authority; but then there are some who received *grants* (that is, gifts) from the state of North Carolina.

We spent the night at Mary'sville in a new public house, but with honest folk who treated us very well. The host is called Mr Burk. It is not the best looking of inns but is, I think, very comfortable; the other one was full.

Between Knox and Mary'svilles we noticed a cave that they told us was very deep, but full of standing water that limits entry to thirty paces or so. We did not go inside.

After Mary'sville the countryside becomes prettier again. It is flatter, and there seemed to be fewer streams. The woods are more sparse, that is, the trees are not so thickly clumped. They spring up over very beautiful, very lush grass. There are excellent meadows here that could be mowed as they are. The closer to the Tennassee River, the better the land. The region's lushness has attracted several colonists, who settled here despite the proximity of uncontested Cherokee territory, but they are going to lose their homes as soon as the line is drawn.

Some miles from the Tennassee we saw a spring that runs under the road, flowing beneath boulders that make a sort of miniature natural bridge like Virginia's.

We came to *Tellico Bloc House*,[19] also called *Fort Wilkinson*. We were warmly welcomed by Mr Strother, the lieutenant commanding the

[19]The Tennessee Valley Authority is currently attempting to restore a village and a trading post at Tellico as they would have looked in the eighteenth century.

garrison, and at dinner we ate wild turkey for the first time. It is a bit dryer than the domesticated bird, but otherwise the same meat with almost the same taste.

We saw a great many interesting people upon our arrival, for there are always a large number passing the time of day here. Independently of Mr Strother we found Mr Dinsholm, the United State's Cherokee agent, and some other people more or less familiar with Indian customs. The conversation turned on that subject, which was a real pleasure for us; it is rare enough in these parts to find a topic that yields useful information. I shall set down what I learned there, and in the region generally, and also what I saw with my own eyes. South of the Ohio and east of the Mississippi there are four Indian (I prefer that word to *savage*, much used among us, because I do not find that these people merit that epithet in any way) nations* which form three quite distinct tribes. The Cherokees and the Chickasaws are the two northern nations of this area, plus the Creeks and the Choctaws. I preserve here the English spelling, which is a fairly literal imitation of the Indian word. I have had the Indians pronounce the names of the two northern nations for me and they said, with their choppy accent, *Tchero-Khi, Tchikeso.*[20] I consider these four nations

---

*Creeks is a generic term applied by the English to the nations which were better known to the French as Machecoux, Talapours, Apalaches, etc.

[20]The Duc d'Orléans, who always tried to learn the language of a country in which he spent any time, and was polyglot like most of the princes of his period, did not miss this chance to pick up some Cherokee dialect, related to the Iroquois, during these few days in an Indian area. His brother Beaujolais makes droll allusion to it in a letter to their sister Adelaide, 21 April 1803: "A fine bunch of babblers we'll be when we're all together again.

only three tribes: the Choctaws and the Chickasaws, their neighbors along the Mississippi, speak absolutely the same language barring a few unimportant words. I have that fact among others from Major Colbert, of whom I shall have more to say and who is himself a Chickasaw. This identity of language extends to usage also, and has established a tight alliance and a firm friendship between these two peoples, who cannot remember a breach of either. Latterly they have followed a different policy from the other nations living near the whites east of the Mississippi, and have taken no part in the Indian wars against the United States from Florida to Canada.* So I can only consider the Chickasaws and Choctaws one people, as they have evidently a common origin.

These people's complexion is a yellow-black, though their skin color seems to me less yellow than mulattoes' and yet no deeper black.** Some claim that the four nations who live south of the Ohio are a bit darker than those north of it, but most people have assured me that if seen together they would be indistinguishable. It is impossible to be sure whether or not these groups originated where they now live. Their famous traditions are too recently developed to allow

Mama will speak Spanish, you German, Chartres Cherokee, Montpensier a delightful medley."

After the Cherokees they visited other "savage" nations, all of which welcomed them warmly. They found the Indians "infinitely more hospitable than the Americans of the Back Countries."

*Some of them have even served in the American army.

**It is a rule that the farther south one goes the darker the natives' complexion.

of certain knowledge. We may judge the youth of these traditions by the absence of any notion about the Europeans' arrival on their continent. And there seem to be great disparities among them. The Cherokees believe that they are natives of a distant land west of the Mississippi and much farther south than their present home. Winters

Choctaw Eagle Dance. George Catlin. MUSEUM OF THE NEW-YORK HISTORICAL SOCIETY.

were much shorter and warmer there than here. I am told they claim to have crossed the Mississippi and ravished this region from another tribe which they drove out.

I have also heard an odd story which I cannot vouch for, though I have had it from several people. There exists west of the Mississippi an Indian nation people call *the Welsh Indians* who have retained enough of the speech of Wales to make themselves understood in that language.* It is said that their children are born as white as whites, and if the adults are darker than we, the change is due solely to the heat of the sun. There is considerable uncertainty as to how a Welsh or European colony could have reached the area. Some identify them as the remains of a colony sent out from England to the Mexican coast, which was shipwrecked, they say, west of the Mississippi. I intend to look into this when I reach home. (Since then I have had reason to believe it only a tall story.)

By and large Indians are not strong, but they say the young ones are nimble and agile. They say the lack of strength derives from their diet, but I believe otherwise; I think it is rather a result of the humidity, the variable climate, and the summer heat. One fact reported to me seems to prove that their nourishment is even better than our own: during the last war the bodies of Indians killed in battle were still fresh when the Americans' were already rotting. I believe the Americans' immoderate consumption of whiskey accelerates putrefaction. The southern Indians would also indulge to excess if they

---

*But it appears that this is a false report.

could procure whiskey, but they cannot distill it and outsiders sell them very little. Americans, who never walk if they can ride, consider the Indians famous hikers, but I doubt that they would seem so good beside our better European marching men. I believe that on this point, as on so many others, the supposed superiority of the Indians is only by comparison to the Americans, and would vanish if they were measured against Europeans, who are, it seems to me, if not stronger at least more vigorous, active, and enterprising than the Americans. Their longevity is about the same as the Americans' and some that we have seen were quite old. Moreover, they suffer all our diseases and afflictions and have different ways of treating them. I have been assured that they cure all sorts of venereal disease radically and quickly with plants. No one could tell me which plants.

None of these Indians profess any formal religious creed. Nonetheless, they believe that there is *The Great Man Above* who made everything here below, but they are too lazy to pursue that idea further and too refractory to be strict about ceremonies or religious duties. (Certainly they observe a few practices or rituals unfamiliar to us. They are very reluctant to describe such activities, or even to identify them, but they do observe rites that each of us may interpret for himself.)

Marriage is unknown among them (that is, in our meaning of the word).[*] An Indian may take as many wives as he can feed; he takes

---

[*] I have learned since that there were ceremonies of marriage, varying with the tribe. These ceremonies consist of races, dances, or various games.

them on and turns them away like servants, and similarly they leave him when it suits them to do so. Although this custom is widespread among them, chastity and jealousy are known in some tribes. The Creeks show excessive jealousy and strictness on this point. They cut off adultresses' ears upon slight consideration, and do the same to strangers who fall under suspicion. Also, their women never serve men directly; they set the object on a table and the men cannot touch it until the women have withdrawn. The Choctaws and Chickasaws are also very strict on this point, but not as much so as the Creeks. The Cherokees, on the other hand, are exceedingly casual. If a Cherokee's woman sleeps with another man, all he does is send her away without a word to the man, considering it beneath his dignity to quarrel over a woman. And all Cherokee women are public women in the full meaning of the phrase: dollars never fail to melt their hearts.

It is notable that this freedom of concubinage, this polygamy, invariably renders the women contemptible in men's eyes and deprives them of all influence. That is an awkward forecast for Frenchwomen; new divorce laws have made their marriage an Indian concubinage. It is quite true that women can free themselves from the dependence due to their weakness only by the nobler feelings they arouse in men, and not by the pleasures they offer. If these pleasures are not to degrade the emotions, they must serve exclusively to heighten the affections of a man who loves and believes himself loved. But if they are lavished on legions, the magic of the emotion vanishes, and women fall into degradation and thence into dependence. But back to my story: the Indians have all the work done by women. They are assigned not only household tasks; even the corn, peas, beans, and potatoes are planted, tended, and preserved by the women. The man smokes peacefully while the woman grinds corn in a mortar (this mortar is no more than a hollowed tree trunk, and the pestle is a long piece of wood, one end about as wide as the hollow).

Like all the Indians hereabouts, the Cherokees have a governing council, this council being composed of chiefs. In this nation the number of chiefs is not fixed. The council sees to its own successors and usually chooses them from the same families, unless the sons of chiefs are dim-witted, or otherwise unqualified. This council can make war and peace, conclude treaties, and pass laws. As there is no written language, the laws are not imperishable, but they are enforced with great rigor until they are forgotten. The council recently passed a law on theft. For the first offense, flogging, and for the second, the ears cut off. This law has already been applied, and they say that those thus punished are thenceforth scorned by the others. These chiefs command the army and direct the main operations, but there are many private expeditions to pillage houses or isolated farms. In their armies the warriors stay, go, and return just as they please; no one cares. Their ways in war are fierce; they rarely take prisoners. In the last war they took some who were, most of them, transported to Detroit after being dragged all over the region, and were then sold to Canadian traders who resold them to Americans. Usually they do not scruple to massacre women and children. John Watts is singled out because he never killed a woman or child, though he has slain 30 to forty people. They say that during an unsuccessful attack on one of the Cumberland stations, one of the chiefs (whom I also saw) called *Double-Head* offered to circle around behind to massacre the women and children and wipe out the settlers' families. John Watts urged the chiefs to reject the idea and won. However frightful and revolting these methods, we can understand what has driven the Indians to such cruelty: a massacre does irreparable harm to their enemy. They even say that they no longer know how to deal with the whites, because deaths occasioned among Indians by the whites are irremediable and cannot be made up, while white losses are made up immediately and nothing stops their expansion into the region. We must be fair: the whites' systematic spoliation of the Indians has not even slowed. All the Indians' neighbors are greedy for their Tennassee territories. The last treaty[21] has aroused serious discontent among the whites, who would like a war with the Indians so a new treaty can strip them of the coveted lands. Four months ago the whites assassinated two Indians (one a chief called Red Bird), hoping that the provocation would lead to reprisals and trigger a war. The Indians demanded the surrender of the murderers. This was refused on the pretext that they should not be yielded over to Indian torture, and that according to the treaty they must be judged by American law. The whites promised to conduct an investigation and have the murderers punished, but it would seem that nothing of the

---

[21]It is hard to tell which treaty is meant. During the Revolution, Americans warred on the Indians of the Great Lakes region who were allied with the English, beginning in July 1777. There were many alliances with tribes and even with confederations of tribes.

sort was done. I heard one of the assassins identified, so it would not be hard to find them. In the meantime, as nothing was done, the Cherokees assassinated four whites, and as nothing was said, all has been calm since.

People always count Indian populations by *warriors*, that is, by *men capable of bearing arms*. Every man comes up with his own count, mainly according to his own interests or wishes. Some tell me that the Cherokees were so depleted by the last war that they would have trouble raising 500 warriors. Others claim they have 2,000, still others 1,000, 1,200, 1,500, etc. I presume that the last two figures are closest. The Chickasaws are usually estimated at 500 or 700 warriors, but there is wide disagreement about the Creeks and the Choctaws.* Generally they told me the Choctaws were more numerous. The most common estimate seemed to be ten to eleven thousand, and about eight or nine thousand Creeks (if we count as Creeks the diverse, though loosely united, tribes I spoke of, people say there are as many of them as there are Choctaws).

Ownership of the land is in common among all Indians, but they acknowledge the individual ownership of crafted things and movable goods like corn, beans, horses, bulls, cows, etc. They even recognize the ownership of Negroes and their descendants. Many of them own slaves, which they buy and sell as is done in Virginia and Carolina. According to one clause of the treaty the Indians are required to return local Negroes who escape, and they have done so often.

*This disagreement is easy to explain: those nations, farthest off, are less familiar to the Americans.

Pawnee. George Catlin. MUSEUM OF THE NEW-YORK HISTORICAL SOCIETY.

There are many whites living among the Indians. All they have to do is take an Indian wife (or several if it suits them) and serve in the army in case of war. Aside from that they can live as they please and do anything that does not violate Indian law. Among the Cherokees and, I believe, among all Indians, the family is reckoned around women rather than around men as in our society. They claim that only motherhood is sure. In consequence, the children of white men and Indian women are Indians like the others. The Americans call them *half breeds*. They live precisely as the others do, neither read nor write, and ordinarily speak only the tribal tongue. There are some, however, who can make themselves understood in English, and report has it that they are a bit more intelligent than the others. John Watts is an Indian of that sort; his father was an Englishman, a captain in an English regiment. He was sent to Cherokee country by his government, and liking the way of life, took an Indian woman and settled down. His son John Watts is the nation's greatest warrior and is considered the most influential of the chiefs. But there is one who outranks him in administrative matters. He is the one they call *Little Turkey-Cock*. It is he whom the Indians always declare great chief of the nation, but others claim that this is only for form's sake and appearances, and that Watts is indeed the dominant chief whose views always prevail in council. During my stay at Tellico I dined with Little Turkey-Cock, but he does not speak English so I found chatting rather a trial and was obliged to use an interpreter (an Irishman named Carey settled among the Cherokees for these 30 or 40 years). *Bloody Fellow* is another of the great war chiefs.

The American government maintains several agents among the Southern Indians, under the direction of the Superintendent of Southern Indians, Colonel Hawkins, and the War Department. We were received with marked courtesy by Mr Dinsmore, the Cherokee agent. He lives in their territory 90 miles from Tellico Bloc House and runs no more risk than any ambassador, for the Indians hold his office in respect, and in case of a break between the Cherokees and the United States, he would be escorted to the frontier by his hosts, as he would in civilized countries.

The government maintains other agents, independent of these, at Tellico Bloc House, who run a store on its behalf. This trading post is intended to supply the Indians with various goods they may need. Payment is by money, or by hides, or by other commodities that can be resold in the east. The object is, I am informed, to supply the Indians with the necessary merchandise at as low a cost as possible short of actual loss, and thus to teach them the value of our goods, to preserve them from a fleecing by the private merchants who traffic with them. These latter require special permission of the United States government, and obtain it with no trouble. The only forbidden commodity—even the trading post supplies it only very rarely and in minuscule quantities—is liquor. The innkeeper at Tellico is even forbidden to keep a single drop in his house. These precautions are very praiseworthy and very wise in all respects.* I have often had occasion to travel some miles in the company of these traders, and consequently to chat with them about their business, which must be profitable. They sell mainly light fabrics, linens, and hardware; needles are worth more than money. But Indians know what money is,

*Note that they will sell the Indians as much powder and shot as they want, or are able, to buy.

and what it is worth, and often accept it in payment, though they prefer barter for the goods they need. The traders take payment in hides, furs, often in livestock that they sell later in the east, etc. The Indians trade a little with Mobile too, and even with New Orleans; it is mainly from the latter place that they acquire whatever liquor they manage to pick up. The traders say it is easy and even pleasurable to travel among them. Aside from the hospitality lavished on them wherever they appear, they can buy the necessities of life for extremely modest prices; I heard they could buy a pig for a quarter of a dollar or the equivalent.

Tellico Bloc House is a compound formed by a stockade of thick trees split in two and planted like huge hedgerows. The space between the trunks makes loopholes, and Mr Strother told me that was the best possible fortification against the Indians and commanded as much respect as a true fortress. All the same, the Indians have captured a few of these fortresses, and old Fort Loudon, of which more shortly, is a nearby example.

Tellico Bloc House contains living quarters for a detachment of 60-odd American infantry, the commandant, and the traders, as well as the trading post itself. On the heights near Tellico they are going to build a fort to be named Fort Wilkinson after the general of that name.[22] It will be just like all forts in Indian territory. I shall describe these forts when I have seen those in the western area. This is one

[22] Almost certainly General James Wilkinson (1757–1825), a conspirator and adventurer, who re-entered active service in 1791 to fight Indians.

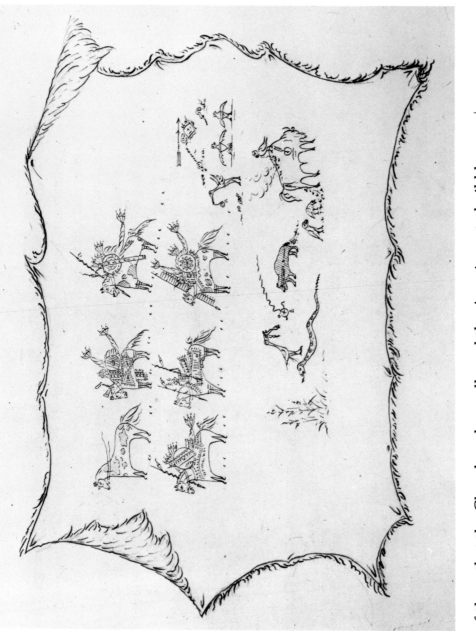

Facsimile of a Pawnee doctor's robe.
George Catlin. MUSEUM OF THE NEW-YORK
HISTORICAL SOCIETY.

of three that the Cherokees have allowed the Americans to build by the latest treaty. The two others are Fort Granger and Fort Hamtranck at the confluence of the Holstein and the Clinch. The site of Fort

Wilkinson seems well chosen, though it may be vulnerable from the high ground on the far bank of the river. They say that is merely an effect produced by the trees. Perhaps; just the same I think high ground across the river from the fort would make it hot for the defenders if they were besieged by regular troops.

Fort Loudon was built on the left bank of the Tennassee, and if they had not told me so, I should never have imagined that anyone would set a fort on a spot like that. It is vulnerable on all sides, and with the river behind it, supplies could be cut off easily. That is what happened, by the way, in the Seven Years' War.[23] The British garrison of five hundred men was forced to capitulate after suffering all the horrors of famine and holding out for six weeks. By the terms of surrender they were to lay down their arms, deliver up all stores, and withdraw unmolested; but they were massacred by the Cherokees after covering a few miles on the other side of the river (some say through betrayal, some because they hid ammunition), and only a small advance guard, marching some distance before, escaped. Some perished, so they say, after unspeakable tortures. The enemy drove thick splinters of richly resinous pine into their flesh and then set fire to them! One shudders at the thought. And yet these same Cherokees, so cruel in war, have a horror of human flesh and any who eat it.

There is a ferry across from Tellico Bloc House where a few soldiers

---

[23]The French and Indian War, between the British colonists on one side and the French and Indians on the other, began in 1754. In 1756, it spread to Europe, where it was called the Seven Years' War.

of the garrison are always detailed to carry Indians, who pay nothing, back and forth. As a result there are always many Indians in the fort. The commandant's office is usually full of them. As long as the door is open they enter without formalities, shake the right hand of anyone and everyone in the room, then sit down and smoke tranquilly. It goes on like that all day long, unless the commandant indicates that he wishes to do some writing. In that case they all go out, and by closing his door the commandant is sure of peace and quiet as long as it suits his convenience, but when the door is opened they troop right in again and take possession of the room.

Either because the habit of hearing English has taught them a few words or sounds by which they recognize that language, or because our appearance differed from the Americans', we had not been in the room above a quarter hour when they realized that we were not American. Among themselves they repeated the word *squouannah* several times, meaning *Spanish*, and pointed at me while repeating the word on an interrogatory tone. Apparently my swarthy complexion, untrimmed beard, and unpowdered hair lent me a Spanish air; but what surprised me greatly was the speed of their discovery that we were not American. As soon as I knew what they meant, I disabused them of the notion, and it was explained to them that we were *Krenché*, that is, *French*. They continually supply Tellico with game, eggs, fruits in season, etc., so that the Tellico market is always well stocked, and it is certainly one of the best forts in the region. The availability of women makes it very pleasant for the soldiers. Just now there is an abundance of strawberries, which the women and girls bring in and sell at ninepence the gallon. I noticed that these strawberries, all wild, were of the hautboy variety. Soon there will be watermelons of an exquisite fragrance, much like the fragrance of pineapples, they say. A 20-pound wild turkey sells for one shilling at the moment, and other sizes proportionately. Mr Strother, the commandant, did us the kindness to ask the chiefs to put on a ball game for us tomorrow, which they did not much care for, having played several games in recent days for the entertainment of the boundary commissioners. But six gallons of spirits that we promised the winners decided the matter, and it was agreed that there would be a ball game at two in the afternoon.

In the morning we crossed the river with Mr Strother and went first to the site of Fort Loudon, which is buried under brush now, with only a little rubble and a few irregularities of terrain to commemorate the fort's existence. Nearby, on the same level, an Indian has built his shack, or rather his house, as it looks very much like all the houses of the poor around here. The main difference is that the latter are a bit squatter and a bit smaller, and instead of selecting good thick trunks for construction, they took thin ones and small, because they were less trouble to cut down and transport. They stuff the chinks with a mastic made of earth and sand, as our peasants do.* The door is extremely narrow, but high enough to enter without stooping. When we went in, the men were eating a soup of cornbread and milk.

*Their roofs too are like our peasants', with stones laid on strips of bark, as in Switzerland and on all wooden houses.

83

They offered us some immediately, according to the rules of Indian hospitality. Their spoons were wooden and fairly well made. In shape they were more pointed and triangular than ours. The fire was at one end of the room in a fireplace like our own, and the beds, made of slats laid the long way and covered with blankets, stood against the long wall. This Indian's house is in a pretty setting; stretching out before him he has a vast green carpet that ends in wooded hills, and on the horizon mountains that distance has tinted blue.* To his left he looks out at the river, flowing so serenely that it seems a lake, the island nearby, and the sloping riverbank. Later we crossed the plain that lay before us, passed through some beautiful country, and came to another house with a truly picturesque setting. It is of the same sort that I have just described, but a few low, bushy trees beside it make it even prettier. On the whole I have not yet seen untilled land that looked less like a wilderness than this. One can see entire treeless plains that could be mowed just as they are. The river is lined with various kinds of acacias and with catalpas, chestnut trees, wild vines, and trees unknown to our continent, all of which grace this part of the country with the aspect of one of our English gardens. Almost always the Indians plant a few fruit trees outside their houses, like peach trees or apple trees. Our guide entered every house, and when the husbands or fathers were distracted, he made no effort to disguise his little *games* with the wives or daughters; and they were so little embarrassed that one of them who was lying on a bed put her hand

---

*The Alleghanys or Appalachians.

on his trousers before my very eyes and said scornfully, *Ah, sick.* Some of these Indian women are quite lovely, and I was struck by their flirtatious ways; they are very different from their neighbors, and no Frenchwoman could teach them a thing.

There is nothing unusual about their clothes, except perhaps for the way they wrap themselves in a blanket, in one fold of which they carry their babies on their backs as if in a basket. They all wear a band about their hair, close to the head, and sometimes braid the hair. Some, but not many, wear earrings; I saw none with a nose ring. Their garments, like the men's, are all made of our European materials, and their blankets too. They have red ones, blue ones, embroidered, etc. . . . I even saw a few women who had painted their faces with vermilion, using it artfully and pleasingly.

We followed the trail that leads through this lovely region to Tôkona. *Tôkona* is a Cherokee village about three miles from Tellico Bloc House. (I note that I write Tôkona, lacking a better way to set down the Indian sounds; the last vowel is not a pure *a* but an *a* modified toward an *o*.) Before entering the village, we stopped on a man-made hillock to take in the view. The village stands in a beautiful setting, rendered even more beautiful by a pellucid sky.

There are no more than eight or ten houses at the most in Tôkona. They are laid with some symmetry and at measured distances around what the Indians call in English, *town house.* The houses form not a circle but a parallelogram. They are just like those I have described. The town house is a special sort of building. It is a circular wooden structure but entirely thatched, so to speak, covered all over by reeds

85

and corn husks. It looks much like the flour mills in our own grain-growing regions. The only difference is that the Indian town houses (at least the ones I saw) are much broader at the base and therefore seem lower, though I believe the height is about the same.* The entrance is to the south; it is a narrow, low corridor, constructed like the rest of the building but with a hollowed-out half tree trunk for a roof. This corridor is at most five feet high and we had to stoop to enter. It is no more than six or seven feet long. It ends before a reed screen, and we had to take a few steps to the right to enter the main room. As there is no window or opening except that entrance, the interior is very shadowy and cool. It was impossible to see anything when we first entered, and for some minutes we were in complete gloom. Gradually our eyes adapted and we saw that we were in a hexagonal room. At its center is the hearth where they lay a fire in winter. Each face of the hexagon (always excepting those that serve as doorway or hide the main entrance) is a little alcove with a reed bench. On the three pillars facing the inner entrance hang the three ceremonial shields of the three Cherokee tribes. *The serpent, the tortoise, and the lizard* are their emblems. Each of these animals, distinctly recognizable, is painted in black, on an octagonal shield, white with a black border dotted white. These shields are wooden and are hung from the posts just below the roof, as the shields of medieval knights in tournaments are depicted. When the Indians foregather in their town houses they usually take their places in the proper tribal nook.

*The exterior walls are very low and the roof begins about three feet off the ground.

These compartments are about four feet deep and their height at the wall about seven feet. I estimate the diameter of the hexagon at about 30 feet. There is no carpet or anything like one; the earth is simply tamped and leveled. The Indians never tear down a town house, but when it collapses from sheer decrepitude or for other reasons, they

View of the Cherokee Indian village at Tokono, on the banks of the Tennessee, which the princes visited 1 and 2 May 1797. Lithography from a painting by Storelli (1819) inspired by a painting by Montpensier (1804), both lost. PHOTO, SERVICE PHOTOGRAPHIQUE DES ARCHIVES NATIONALES.

bury it under earth and mud and build one just like it in another spot. The artificial hill from which we first saw Tôkona was so made. The middle of its summit has settled a bit, and it looks just like a truncated cone. To one side are a few trees, and it was from there that Montpensier sketched the village.

Examining the structure, and absorbing the details I have just reported, I thought this building must be consecrated to some form of worship. I could infer no other reason for the Indians' reverence and the care with which they buried the debris, but everyone insisted that they had no formal religion and that these town houses were only for their meetings, in cold weather or hot. There they dance in single file, circling the fire, and from the imitation I saw, I can best compare them to our old *passepieds*. * Often they lodge strangers and travelers in the town house.

Almost all the open land in Tôkona is cultivated in their fashion, which is to clear only the spot where they plan to sow or plant each stand of corn or bed of potatoes, etc. They dig their holes and plant. Grass grows up around the spot, and they only weed out what is close enough to the plant to harm it directly. This is certainly a less exhausting method than most; but seeing the fields that result, one would not believe that they had been cultivated at all. They grow only corn, potatoes, and tobacco.

We went to one house where we saw a group of Indian men seated,

*Since then I have seen the real thing. It is rather like *la cosaque*, and they keep pointing their toes in and out as they go.

smoking, while the women worked inside. We went right up to the men and shook hands, which they did firmly without rising or disturbing themselves in any way. Then the first to light his pipe invited everyone else to puff at it before he did; such is Indian courtesy, and when we lit our own we too were careful to have all the others take a puff. We were smoking what the Cherokees call *Taluma*, the Chickasaws *Mositchek*, some northern Indians *Kaltikinek*, etc. The Americans call it *Little Shoemake* to distinguish it from *Big Shoemake*, which is what we call *sumac*, and the American French call *Appapona*. I believe that it is a separate species. They harvest the shrub's leaves in autumn after the sun has burned it dry and the frost has nipped it. It is exceedingly pleasant to smoke.[24] The Indians smoke it straight or mixed with tobacco. They also smoke the shrub's berries and the bark of the little red willow. They use two kinds of pipe. One is at the end of a hatchet, and the handle serves as stem. That is what they

[24]Bernard de Marigny, who had entertained the three princes in New Orleans in 1797 and had lent them 1,000 piastres, kept in touch with the Duc d'Orléans, as did his family. Doubtless recalling pipes and cigars smoked in his company, in August 1822 de Marigny sent him a gift of sixty kilos of plug tobacco, one kilo of fine cut tobacco, and a buffalo hide. In August 1827 his son Gustave was in Paris, probably studying at the École Spéciale Militaire, and was often received at the Palais-Royal.

One of the last letters signed by Louis-Philippe was his reply of 10 August 1850 to the son of his quondam host, who, hearing the king was in poor health, had written to him from New Orleans on 15 July 1850: "I hope, Sire, that if one of your sons comes to America he will visit Louisiana; your friend of fifty-two years is still there. I could not receive him as my father did you, for I am without great wealth, a head clerk who once had millions; but my long and sincere friendship will make up for much, in their eyes, and will be of value. . . ." One branch of the de Marigny family remained in France, that headed by Vice-Admiral Charles Bernard de Marigny (1740–94).

call a *tomahawk*. The other is made of a soft stone that they work themselves, the stem being the stalk of a shrub found only in this region. Some are sculpted with scenes of every imaginable depravity. They brought me one with a bear and a wolf on it and named me *Atota*, that is, "father." It is one of their customs to name strangers that way. Mr Strother is called *Kananoa*, that is, "Pipe." Mr. Dinsmore, who is thin and lanky and taller than I, is called, I don't know why, "Jonah the Bear." Another is called "Bench." And so forth. For two dollars I bought the hide of a *mink* (English word), which is a small otter. It was stitched up to make a tobacco pouch, decorated with red-dyed horsehair and full of taluma. Similarly I acquired a belt embroidered Indian fashion, and Mr Strother made me a gift of a pair of garters and a pipe.

We went into one house where there were strawberries, which they offered immediately; also they served us very good cornbread with beans cooked into it. The woman called this bread *gâto*, pronouncing the *o* very clearly. I thought it was an obvious imitation of our *gâteau*, but I have no idea how it entered the Cherokee language. The interpreter assured me that this word *gâto* was their word for that kind of bread. Hospitality is the rule among all Indians. All their guests make free with anything in sight, and they imagine that matters are the same with us, so that without actually stealing, they help themselves to whatever lies loose. They smoked our pipes any time they could lay hands on them. Any man's tobacco and taluma are always available to all without offer or permission. Helped along by such hospitality, some Indians have traveled widely. Mr Strother told me there are Cherokees who have been as far as New Spain. When they take a notion to travel, they saddle and bridle a horse, roll their blankets, and leave without further ado. Truly nothing is freer or happier than these Indians. Though they all have horses, they make no use of them in their wars. Only one small tribe, on the banks of the Missouri, customarily fights on horseback, armed with slings as well as big knives. That tribe is called the *Panis* [Pawnees]. Some say their horses are of Spanish origin, others insist that they are native to the American continent and that large herds of wild horses still roam west of the Mississippi. They all spring from domesticated stock; at least that is my belief.

We sat smoking with the Indians for some time, and then returned to Tellico where we dined with Mr Strother. The open country and cleared areas I saw are largely ravages wrought by the Americans in their wars with the Cherokees.

After dinner we crossed the river again with two hogsheads of whiskey, the garrison's drum, and a crowd of Indians, one or two of whom spoke English. We bore the two hogsheads in triumph onto the battlefield where all was being readied for the ball game.[25] The Indians called it *Hannatsökë*, with a long *o* and a very distinct last syllable. Ordinarily the game is preceded by a challenge from one team to the other, then come the *war cry*, the *scalping cry* (for slicing off the skin over the skull, hair attached, which they keep as a trophy), and finally the *death cry*. As there had recently been several

[25]Many Indian tribes play this ball-and-racket game.

Hannatsóké and they were a bit tired, they started without all those preliminaries, to my deep regret. The story goes that for an inspired and exciting game, they have to wager among themselves, and unfortunately that is just what did not happen.*

Before beginning, all the players strip down to a belt with a little square of cloth before, red, yellow, etc., hemmed in another color, and the same behind; which is called a breechclout. These two squares of cloth are tied together below in such a way that while they do not appear fastened, no indecencies are possible. That is their combat uniform, and they never wear more in war. Each player is armed with two rackets, crude versions of our tennis rackets. But they are narrower than ours and concave; you will see why. There is less string than in ours and it is fairly slack. There is only one ball for the whole game. Each team defends one goal line.** The ball is tossed up at center, where the players always begin by leaping in en masse, whacking rackets together in a scramble for the ball. Usually it falls to the ground and there is another battle of rackets for possession. Finally the one who comes up with it holds it between his two rackets, carries it off or at least passes it toward the goal line; victory

*To understand this game you must picture a field with lines at either end like goal lines. The center of the field is marked and there is an intermediate point, on either side, between the center and the end line. The players are divided into two equal teams; ours were of twelve men, twenty-four altogether. There were eight players, four from each team, at center. Four stationed evenly on each of the other points along the lines.

**About a third of the players take positions in the center, and the others in various groupings toward the goal lines. The two teams oppose each other all over the field, often snaring the ball on their own goal line and carrying it all the way to the opponents'.

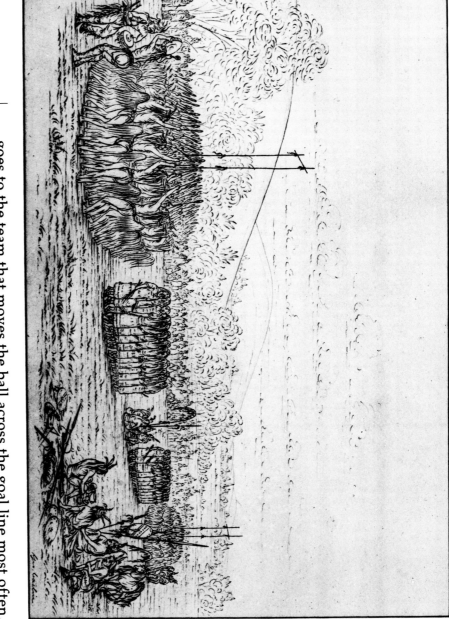

Choctaw Ball-Play Dance. George Catlin. MUSEUM OF THE NEW-YORK HISTORICAL SOCIETY.

goes to the team that moves the ball across the goal line most often. So one team will try to gain possession to pass it if not over, then at least in the general direction of the goal line, and the other tries to capture it and bring it back the other way. As soon as the ball crosses a goal line the offensive team scores *one* and the ball is brought back to center for another toss. The first team to score 12 wins. The game sparks race after race and shows off the savages' agility. It is highly suspenseful as well, for I have seen the ball picked up almost at one goal line and played all the way back to the other. If the player who has snared the ball is slow in passing it, he stands a good chance of losing it, and no holds are barred in taking it away from him. They start by chasing him, and if they catch him before he has thrown it, that is his hard luck; they buffet one another mercilessly and produce horrible spills; some have seen men killed on the spot. What is most admirable is that neither during the game nor afterward is there ever the least argument. During play no one says a word; the chiefs and spectators keep score, and as soon as the game ends the losers disappear, the winners carry off the prizes, and in a moment the battlefield is deserted. The game that I saw went to 11–10.

We went back to Tellico immediately afterward. On the far bank we could hear the good cheer and shouts inspired by the whiskey. They hollered long and vainly for the ferry, and Mr Strother posted three sentries instead of one. Finally two ambassadors arrived in a small canoe, bearing the two empty hogsheads and demanding more, presenting *Little Turkey-Cock*'s belt and banner as credentials. They were told that the commandant was asleep and the trading post closed; they went away calmly and we heard nothing more about it until the next morning, and then all they did was show us in sign language that they had drunk a bit too much the night before.

Often we saw Indians paddling along in a canoe made of a hollow tree (as in Switzerland but better made). They all stand up in them, and some play a kind of flute that they make by cutting holes in a thick hollow reed. Though crude, it is lovely to hear at a distance across the water, especially when the freshness and novelty of the scene embellish every sight and sound.

Cherokee clothing is made with European cloth and goods. The rich among them wear ample dressing gowns in bright prints or similar cloth. Some wear hats, but the majority keep the Indian haircut. They shave everything but the skull and the back of the head, and look as Capuchin monks would look if they let the hair grow inside their aureoles. The fringes of their hair are usually decorated with a few hanging tokens or braids in their style, and banded by a piece of tin or red-dyed horsehide. Sometimes the hair itself is dyed red with vermilion, which is frightful and makes them look all bloody. On the whole, vermilion is very stylish among them, and is always applied where you would least expect to find it: now a thick dab under one eye and nowhere else, now one in front of the ear, now one at the roots of the hair. Some prink by twining wild turkey feathers, or other birds', in their hair, and attaching fobs to them, or little bits of glass, or red-dyed goose down.

Their clothing is so various that an exact description is impossible. Most wear a woollen blanket over the left shoulder and beneath the right, so as to leave the right arm entirely free. They all wear a shirt or tunic which is, I am told, washed fairly often. They bathe fairly often. Trousers, breeches, or underpants are unknown to them. They have only the little square of cloth, and the shirt or tunic is belted in and hides it altogether.

Some are turned out with notable elegance, and I saw one among many (him I bought the pouch from) whose outfit consisted of silk fichus and a light green cape or length of cloth, which hung with classic elegance and charm.

The outer rim of the ear is always slightly detached by an incision. They wrap it in a layer of tin and from it hang very long, very large earrings. Often too they hang a little triangle or other ornament through the nasal septum. These embellishments are reserved to the men.

The Louisiana French call the *Cherokees Cherakis.*

May 3d we left Tellico Bloc House, enchanted by Mr Strother's courtesies. Accompanied by Major George Colbert, a Chickasaw on his way home, we took the Cumberland road. We suggested that he guide us to Nashville along the left bank of the Tennassee, so we could see more Indian villages and spend more time among them; but the passage might have been troublesome in its lower reaches, and the major told us that, more particularly, he was afraid some sniper might put a ball through his head. The Cherokees resent the Chickasaws for their neutrality in the last war with the Americans, and they hate the major for several reasons: 1st because with his brothers he served in the American army, 2d because he married a Cherokee woman who owns livestock and is well off, and 3d because they stole two Negroes from him that they do not want to give back. Major Colbert is the son of a Georgian who settled among the Chickasaws with 40 Negroes. These Negroes and their children belong to his family. Father and son served in the American army against the Indians. Some were killed. Father and son earned 50 dollars a month but when peace came their pay was cut off (and it is true that they had left the service before then). In recompense they breveted the one a general and the other a major. The latter is bankrupt because the Creeks, in their war against the Chickasaws, killed off all his livestock, and the Cherokees stole two of his Negroes. He is now on his way home from Philadelphia, where he sought help in vain, at which failure he told the officers discussing the problem that the United States consisted of *damned rascals*. They asked him if the Chickasaws had laws: "*No*," he said, "*you don't need them except for villains and only villains like the Creeks and whites have them.*" He was a good fellow and very obliging. His glimpse of the whites' power had alarmed him, and his knowledge of the language, allowing him to overhear what was being said about the Indians, had only increased that fear. Certainly no effort is made to hide plans to strip the Indians of everything, and their eagerness to get on with it leads the whites often to paint the Indians in false colors. Aside from all that, everyone agrees that our major is a great warrior, so I was all the more surprised to see him easily exhausted. He rode a very gentle horse, but could not stand more than three days' march, and admitted that he was done in. The poor fellow was flat broke, and when I asked him to lend me a quarter one day because I was out of small change, he confessed that he did not have even that much.

Small change is so rare in this area that we have had to cut dollar bills into several triangles for a supply.

We lodged with Judge Campbell, whose house stands on the site of the former Fort Granger, facing the junction of the Holstein and the Tennassee, which makes a little island as it flows in. Unquestionably the Holstein* is the principal river and the Tennassee only a small tributary. A good look at the map[26] had already made me think that the Holstein's volume was far greater than the Tennassee's, and the view from this spot proved it. The Holstein is hardly even swollen by its confluence with the Tennassee, and I cannot conceive why the name Tennassee was given to the merged rivers, unless perhaps as a result of past intent to encroach on the Indians, as it would doubtless have worked to the Indians' advantage if, during the period of early settlement, the Holstein had been generally acknowledged the true Tennassee River. The Holstein was so named after the first colonist to settle on its banks; the other is an Indian name. The Tennassee flows perpendicularly into the Holstein, and the latter's course seems unaffected by the junction. The island in the Tennassee does not even extend past the edge of the Holstein's flow, and is cut off *along a straight line.*

Nothing remains of Fort Granger but a few old stockades. When the commissioners come by they will decide whether or not it is to be rebuilt. Judge Campbell will probably be one of those deprived of

---

*You cross the Holstein by ferry.

[26]We may assume that among the maps they made use of was the *American Pocket Atlas of Mathew Carey*, published in Philadelphia in 1796, which contained nineteen maps together with a concise description of each state. A new edition of this pocket atlas was published in 1801. The two editions are preserved in the Library of Congress, Geography and Map Division, Alexandria, Virginia.

his home by the new boundary. He settled there trusting a warrant from the state of North Carolina, but the state's interpretation of the border treaty differed from the federal government's current version. Of course everyone says it is only a temporary hardship, and that after the first Indian war their property will be restored, and that will not be far off because the Indians can never keep calm for long. In the meantime, the situation rouses great anger against the federal government, and everywhere people are saying that the government's jealousy, its hostility to the western settlements, leads it to maneuver and delay, that it is trying to limit this region's growth, etc. Everyone makes his own sort of threat, and some even talk about pillaging the trading post at Tellico! On the way from Tellico to Judge Campbell's we saw seven or eight very fine plantations and one mill, from which the colonists are about to be expelled. When that operation is completed, the state of Tennessee will not own one inch of land along the river that gives it its name.

We spent the whole afternoon at Judge Campbell's. We were planning to stock up there, but next morning he informed us that he was by no means an innkeeper, that he never accepted money, and that he insisted nevertheless on furnishing us with supplies. We accepted only a flitch of bacon, and he guaranteed that we would find none so good on our journey. Judge Campbell is an intelligent and most courteous man.

The state of Tennessee is that part of North Carolina which declared itself the *State of Franklin* some ten years ago. It was too weak then to maintain itself or compose its quarrel with North Carolina.

99

Carolina ceded it to the United States and it then became the major part of the territory southwest of the Ohio governed by Mr William Blount, today one of Tennessee's senators. It was permanently organized as a state in '96 and drew up a constitution.

On the 4th we left Judge Campbell's despite his, and the boundary commissioners', insistence that we accompany these latter to Cumberland; to these people, who habitually do everything slowly and unceremoniously, it is inconceivable that to save two days a man would renounce the pleasures of leisure, enjoying a borrowed tent and eating better food, but I do not believe there is a European, and above all a Frenchman, who could travel in this region without fretting impatiently for an end to the trip and speeding it up as much as possible. Their amazement reached new heights when they saw us move out despite a few drops of rain; and they repeated that we would not escape from the commissioners, who would make a forced march to catch up with us at the Point and would not let us leave there without them.

Finally we departed. We struck the main road to Knoxville five miles from the Judge's at a spot where there is a little inn, which was fresh out of everything, as are most of the houses scattered along the roads much traveled by migrating families. In the 15 miles from there to the Point, not a single house.

We arrived at night. There is an inn kept by the same man who runs the ferry across the Clinch. A little farther down, about 300

yards, at the confluence* of the Clinch and the Tennassee, is a garrison manned only two months ago. This place is ordinarily called *South West Point*, but they are now building a fort here to be called *Fort Hamtramck*,[27] after a Canadian who has long been in the service of the United States. They are building the fort on a spot marked by the ruins of ancient dwellings. Their traces are few, however; only a few rises and a few excavations can be seen. But a plan is evident, and with much more design than in the Indian projects seen these days. They claim to be following a distinct line of circumvallation between the two rivers, and they say that the rows of adjacent holes within that line were houses and the space between the rows a street. Most striking is a little mound at the highest point. They are leveling it for the construction of the fort. Inside, they found about fifteen skeletons, of which one only had a heavy stone on his head and another on his feet. I have seen several of the bones, which seemed quite well preserved. They had retained their white color, and only the upper part had begun to crumble. On them was none of the mildew I had observed on a skeleton in Norway which had lain in a cave for 900 years. True, the difference in sun and climate may have accounted for the difference in aspect, but the bones here did not seem to me very old. Discussing these points, Captain Wade added a bit of general knowledge, that in 1532 a Spaniard called, if I remember rightly, Don

*The confluence is too far south on the map. It shows fifty miles by water to Judge Campbell's.

[27]Colonel John Francis Hamtramck was a Canadian, a hero of the American Revolution, a "strategist" in General Anthony Wayne's army.

Antonio Pembucci,[28] had come down from Virginia through Tennassee to where New Orleans is today; and Wade feels that the traces now uncovered are the remains of some settlement established by his followers and later destroyed by the Indians. This is all hard to untangle. God knows where and when I shall have time to mull it over. Meanwhile I have been unable to determine whether or not it was a Cherokee custom to set a large stone on their chiefs' heads and another on the feet when they buried them. But I do not believe it was their practice.

Our attempts to stock up at the inn were fruitless. They were, or claimed to be, out of everything. Captain Wade, the garrison commander, to whom we had a letter of introduction, was kind enough to order some small loaves of dry wheat bread baked for us. From the soldiers we bought a little cornbread, some coarse cornmeal, and three or four small chunks of dried beef that would hardly tempt a dog. Besides that we had some corn from Tellico for our horses; and with those provisions and the bacon, we set out through the *Wilderness,* also called the *Desert.* We were supposed to leave in the morning, but the little loaves were not ready and the weather was wretched. That delayed us until noon. We were about to leave when an officer came to announce that the commissioners, their infantry escort, and all their train were about to arrive. At that news we left immediately, despite repeated protestations, while a bull and a pig were slaugh-

---

[28]This seems to be an error, at least in dating. There were no Spaniards in Tennessee at the time. Doubtless the Duc d'Orléans is retailing one of the many legends that proliferated among the Indians, about the presence of a white in their territory.

tered for the commissioners; they were arriving without notice, and had not been expected for two days more. We met the procession between the fort and the ferry. Only one commissioner was there, General Piggins. The two others were bringing up the rear. He renewed his invitations most insistently. We declined as politely as possible, but our refusal struck him as outlandish; here no one can even imagine that a traveler may prefer speed to comfort when not on urgent business. Captain Wade told me that we had passed some nine or ten miles from Westpoint, not far from the cavern we had been told lay nearby. It is very deep and a man can easily penetrate it for 200 paces. A while ago Captain Wade found skulls in there, and heaps of human bones.

We crossed the Clinch on a ferry and rode for several miles through fine country that looked ripe for profitable farming. Eleven miles from the Clinch we started up a fairly steep, fairly tall mountain called *Tennassee Mountain*, because it closes off the Tennessee Valley. Strictly speaking it is even a watershed between the Tennassee and the Cumberland. And yet Cumberland Mountain, which I thought not as high as Tennassee Mountain, stands quite a distance from the Cumberland River. Except for a few spots, the country between the two mountains struck me as poor and arid.

Tennassee Mountain is the tallest I have so far seen in America. But there are no great rock faces, nothing typical of our own mountains. From the summit one descries a great stretch of flat country to the south. Though pleasantly green at this time of year, that plain looks like exactly what it is, namely a vast, empty wilderness, and the sight of it makes an unpleasant and melancholy impression.

Not wanting to halt too early where there was little grass, we pressed on until we could find none at all; and the major persuaded us to camp in the forest near a small stream when he said it was a sure thing (and he was right) that we should not find another for a long way. We built a fire immediately, and after a supper of cornbread, bacon, and two or three wheat biscuits, we slept under our blankets, wrapped in our greatcoats and oilskin cloaks.

The 6th. We went on through the woods for several miles and then made a halt for breakfast in a lovely dell full of tall, thick grass. A copious spring flowed from beneath the boulders we sat on. The place is called *Clabotch*, which is an Indian name. Near where we ate is a low hillock shaded by five or six beautiful trees. The mound is obviously artificial. It is shaped like a truncated cone and is surrounded by a ditch. It rises barely fifteen or sixteen feet. The spot seemed so sweet and agreeable to me that I imagined an Indian village there in the old days, with its town house where the mound stood. But the hillock was too small for that.

After *Clabotch* we crossed a dry, scrubby, sparsely wooded region. The land there is stony. We saw the marks of a fire that consumed several square leagues of forest last autumn. It was sparked by some travelers careless about extinguishing their campfire. All the game fled the area, and though some grass and shrubs have grown in, no wildlife has returned. Otherwise there is more game in this desert than in a hunting preserve at home, and I imagine the Cherokees set great store by it. Here are many bears, deer, some buffalo, few elk. The buffalo has already disappeared from the Cumberland frontier. The local bears seemed to me (at least the bearskins did) smaller than the North European variety. They will not attack men except in defense of their cubs. Men hunt them with hounds. Their last resort is to climb a tree, and rifle fire brings them down.

We found *Obed's river* so high that we had to unload our horses and swim them across, which left us half-soaked for the rest of the day. We were not smart enough to take off our boots and buckskins. This river is not wide, but very rapid. When we camped at night we found some grass for the horses.

The 7th we crossed the Cumberland mountains, which are much lower than the Tennessee mountains, and which do not impede rivers that rise on the northern slope from discharging into the Cumberland River. These mountains are much like all the mountains I have seen in America, that is, a range of dry, stony, rounded hills with none of the great masses that appeal to the imagination. That night we camped on the far side of this range. The soil was already much improved and we found good grass for the horses.

On the 8th we finished our descent from the Cumberland mountains and entered the valley formed by that river. We found marshy terrain covered with tall trees and a species of rushes that grow ten or twelve feet tall with roots (usually as long as the stem) that are the bamboo we at home make walking sticks of. The Americans call this rush *cane*. It grows very thickly, and usually buffalo and bears live deep within the stands. The roads through this cane are terrible. They are swampy; the sun cannot penetrate; they never dry; and with the continual passage of horses and carriages they deteriorate day by day. The land is not as level as might be expected. The traveler goes uphill or downhill almost constantly.

Three miles from the Cumberland River we came to the house of a man called *Anderson*, but he had nothing for our horses, so we pushed on as far as the river, where we hoped for better luck. We crossed it on a ferry by old Fort Blount, which they say is to be rebuilt. There was nothing for our horses but a gallon of corn, which we obtained after many urgent requests. To restore us from the hungers and fatigues of the desert they gave us cornbread, a little milk, and fatback of bear, salted and smoked, which we found impossible to swallow, hungry or no.[29] Beyond Fort Blount we found large cultivated areas, more and more of them as we pushed on. But most of these farms had been settled and planted only the previous autumn, so we found it impossible to buy more provisions than we had, and what we had was not only very bad but also very little. Our horses fasted all day. At night we lodged with a Major Dickson, where we had coffee; he had corn fetched from a neighboring farm.

[29]Later from Sicily, the Duc d'Orléans, in a letter of 1811, lightly recalled the privations he and his brothers had endured: "That reminds me of the advice poor Beaujolais always gave us when we were out of food and money: 'All right, my friends, pinch up the skin of your bellies and dance a *frolane* around the pouch.'" The *frolane* was a Venetian dance, to a very fast rhythm, with one or two couples whirling in a circle.

We fared famously with him, and had two beds for the four of us. This is attractive country, its soil infinitely richer than back east. So many emigrants swarmed in last year that they tallied, I was told, above twenty-four thousand whites and four thousand blacks crossing the Clinch by ferry on their way to the Cumberland. Almost all these emigrants come from North Carolina, a state so arid and unhealthy that people abandon all parts of it in search of good land and a more salubrious climate to the west. The recent peace with the

Louis-Charles d'Orléans,
Comte de Beaujolais.

Indians, promising colonists a spell of tranquility, attracted prodigious numbers of them, so many that shortly they will have nothing to fear from the Indians; on the contrary, they will pose an even greater danger to the Indians, the newcomers' general desire being to strip the tribes of their lands, as has already been done to several in the north. And these immigrants are far from admirable. With their Negroes they bring the obduracy and laziness of slaveowners. These slaves will settle here and by normal increase maintain the ratio, and under such a system I doubt that the region will ever attain the level of culture and prosperity which it certainly favors otherwise. Yet who can predict the strength and permanence of this slave system? It is queer that the savages should have accepted and adopted slaveholding, but with them as with the whites excessive laziness conduced to it. All the Cumberland's tributary *creeks* that we crossed had beds of flat hardpan level as flagstones.

The 9th. Fifteen miles from Major Dickson's and thirty-four from Fort Blount, we entered what is called *The Old Settlement;* meaning that from there to Nashville the colonists have been settled for a longer period. The spot is called *Bletch's lick* (a lick is a salty spring). But no salt whatever is mined from it. The water flows through a hollow tree trunk that someone rammed into place.

Livestock roam about it constantly to lap up the salt water.

The whites first planted sweet corn in the Cumberland Valley in 1779; but the influx of settlers took place later. Nevertheless there are some who have been here fifteen or sixteen years. Only since the last

peace with the Indians, which is to say since two or three years ago, has emigration toward this region increased significantly. One of the considerable drawbacks to the Cumberland Valley is a lack of salt. The springs in the area are not salty enough to be exploited. They say that near where the Cumberland flows into the Ohio there are springs rich enough in salt to supply the deficiency, if anyone cared to develop them. That may be, but it is only a rumor so far. Meanwhile all salt is imported from Kentucky in wagons, and sells for four dollars a bushel, and everyone complains that there is none to be had.

That night we slept at Mr Douglas's, formerly the Somner County courthouse, and on the 10th we reached Nashville at dinner time. Fifteen or sixteen miles out we abandoned one of our horses, which had foundered.

We discovered just how unfortunate our major* was. He was penniless, and if he had not come along with us, I do not know how he would have managed.

In Nashville we lodged at Captain Maxwell's. We would have been comfortable enough there if court had not been in session; as it was, the house was full, and even sleeping on the floor there was hardly room. We spent two full days there to rest our horses and bring our diaries up to date, which was not easy among such a mob. We bought a horse to spell our others. **

_____

*Our major took us two miles out of the way to visit one of his friends, who was not in. We had to swim our horses across fords.

**He was a good one, as in general all horses are in this area, and dirt cheap. [They paid only eighty-five dollars, plus four dollars for shoeing.]

Nashville is much smaller than Knoxville, but infinitely better situated. At most there are sixty houses. The soil is stony or sandy, which would be unfavorable for gardening, but nobody goes to that much trouble around here. They assured me that the Cumberland River was navigable without interruption all the way to its confluence with the Ohio, from a point near where the Kentucky road crosses it. We had a visit from an Englishman called Dr Hennings, who came to invite us to dinner and was exceedingly courteous.

The 13th we left Nashville quite late and made only fifteen miles. We stopped with a man named Briton, as there were no inns farther along. We were more comfortable than we had dared hope.

The 14th we took our midday meal at a stout log-house belonging to Rich. Cavet. We were traveling north from Nashville, following the Kentucky road, which is good generally and a great deal better than the Knoxville–Nashville road. Three miles from Rich. Cavet's stands Major Sharp's house, where we did not stop but which is, they say, a good inn.[30] Approaching it from Nashville the land rises steeply, and beyond Major Sharp's the traveler climbs to the area very incorrectly called *The Barrens* by the Americans. It deserves a special description.

It is a high and dry plateau, where trees are sparse and grass and

---

[30] On 14 May they had an adventure which is not recorded in their diaries but appears in their expense accounts. Their horses ran off and it cost two dollars to have them rounded up.

shrubs plentiful. One sees only small, stunted trees, most of them oaks and hickories, and everywhere lush grass dotted with charming flowers.* So these Barrens struck us as exceedingly pleasant, and were a happy change from the forests we were so weary of. There are some stands of tall timber, but very few and only along the river banks. On the whole the region is quite flat; yet one would be hard pressed to maneuver cavalry there, or even to bring it into battle, because springs or other natural features have dug sinkholes everywhere, and I can best describe the area by suggesting an image of funnels in sand, all on a level. The bottoms of the holes are firm and not at all boggy. The springs we came across were clear and limpid; they were sometimes quite far apart, but people claim that the traveler can always find one near the road by veering either left or right, and I should be rather inclined to credit the assertion, given the lay of the land. The soil on the Barrens struck me as thin but by no means useless, and I think it could be turned to advantage particularly in raising livestock. There are a few marshes but not many, and the traveler's road is always firm. The riverbeds are so deep that I imagine it would be easy to drain the marshes.

After Major Sharp's we crossed sixteen miles of the *Barrens* without a dwelling (except for one new settler fifteen miles from him), and quite late reached Mr Lucas's, where we slept.

The 15th. Still on the Barrens, we rode to Captain Chapman's for

---

*We found excellent strawberries here, and in great quantity.

dinner, and spent the rest of the day there to give our horses another half-holiday. That worthy was alarmed by rumors of war with France. He vilified the American government roundly, stating that it imposed crushing taxes to pay a lot of useless people's salaries, and neglected honest men's political interests scandalously, etc. I made no answer and let him run on. When he finally noticed that I was not participating in the conversation, he told me how strange it was that four Frenchmen like us should be traveling in these lost regions *(back countries)*: that we were put to far too much trouble to be taking any pleasure in it, and that he would not disguise his belief that we had been sent out to incite the Indians to declare war on them. He then added, "Don't do it, because all the poor people are for you now, but they'd turn against you. Plunder the rich, capture their ships, whatever you like. That makes no difference here. But don't rouse the Indians against us. That's what beat the English. Punish the rich Americans who try to cheat France, we won't mind that a bit, we'll even help you; we all hate the American government. All through the west you only hear one opinion: if it was French or even English the government couldn't be any worse than it is now." Patiently I heard out this eloquent discourse, which lasted three-quarters of an hour, and I report it because it is almost word for word what the new settlers and most of the western population said. I answered him simply that if he had any idea what sort of men we were he would never have entertained such suspicions, but that he might now set his mind at ease and rest assured that curiosity alone had brought us here, etc. In the end he apologized, and said to me, "Don't be angry about it. Six months ago I saw a Frenchman come by here botanizing (*hunting some herbs*) and I had the same thoughts but didn't say them aloud; but by golly when I saw the four of you I couldn't control myself, and I had to clear it up."

I should not want to omit here a frank report of what we all witnessed at Captain Chapman's. There were only two beds in the one room that was the house's entire living area, and we were granted only what they call here *house-room*, that is, permission to spread our blankets on the rough planks of the floor, with our bedding arranged so that all four of us lay abreast with our feet to the fire, between the two beds. Captain Chapman got into one bed with his wife, which seemed perfectly straightforward to us. A rather pretty girl who we knew was unmarried got into the other, and that too seemed perfectly straightforward. A strapping young man of about 20 or 22 arrived shortly afterward, while we were settling into our bedding; not standing on ceremony, he undressed and plunked himself into the girl's bed; and while that was indubitably natural, it occasioned a certain surprise on our part. It had no such effect on the captain, who, to relax from the day's fatigues, was enjoying a prose with his wife of which he (though present) were the topic, and in the course of which he found us *odd fellows*, to leave our *home* and undergo all the travail of a painful journey to see deserts, savages, and a thousand other things that a man might reasonably think not worth all the trouble. Nor was he distressed by the young man's intimate manner with his daughter. His other daughter blew out the candle and slipped into the young people's bed, so that the young man was in

113

the middle. That seemed to us even more extraordinary; but the flow of matrimonial conversation abated not a whit. We four paid close attention to these goings-on, and saw to our left, by the gleam of the fire, the young man and the first daughter get up and settle again at the foot of the bed; in a word, we saw all that one can see, while the paternal word-mill continued to grind away as before. And now what do you think of those novels by Crèvecoeur, Brissot, etc.!!!³¹

The 16th. We left Captain Chapman's. We entered a forest through which ran a creek, after having dismounted a while as people always do in the *Barrens* when they strike either a creek or a thick stand of timber. We covered about three miles in these woods and then arrived at the Big Barren River, which we crossed on a ferry. We broke our fast at an unfinished house which will be, I believe, a good inn. Immediately afterward we took up our march again, setting out once more, to our great pleasure, across the beguiling and flowery Barrens. Nothing is more refreshing than a return to those lovely plains after so long a confinement in forests of tall timber, with vision limited to twenty paces. Besides, the grass on the plain is so lush that wherever we stop we can be sure that the horses will find good grazing, and

---

³¹A reference to works offering an ideal vision of life in America. *Letters from an American Farmer,* published in 1783, was the work of Michel-Guillaume Saint-John de Crèvecoeur, a Norman established in the United States.

Jacques-Pierre Brissot de Warville (1754–93), after serving in the Duc d'Orléans' chancellery in 1784, had traveled to the United States in 1788, and then taken a seat on the Left in the Legislative Assembly of 1791. [His associates, who have come down through history as the Girondins, were first called the Brissotins.] He was the author of many books.

that is no small satisfaction to travelers in a region like this. We made fifteen miles on the plains without seeing a house. At the end of that leg we saw, in a dense grove, the house of a newcomer who has been settled here for only six weeks. He gave us white cornbread, which is better than the yellow, and butter and fresh milk, all of which made an exceedingly good dinner. It should be noted that the colonists who come to these barrens always settle in the groves. The forest land is lower, more moist and, according to them, more fertile than the plains. At night we traveled as far as Green River. We slept in the ferry-house. There were no provisions but a little bacon; no butter, no milk, no corn of any kind. The woman of the house told me that about a quarter mile on down we might persuade the householder to have his Negroes mill some corn for us. I went there immediately, and after considerable cajolery my request was granted. They rousted out the two Negroes, who were sleeping in the middle of the room, had them grind some flour for me, and even gave me a little milk. So we supped after a fashion, and next morning at breakfast time the son of the house arrived toting a buck on his back, which supplied us with a splendid breakfast. We took a haunch,[32] against the scarcity of food on the road (which is extreme on all newly settled roads; travelers exhaust the local fare in no time). They say, and I believe them, that this road is already much better than last year. Furthermore, though the lack of provisions is certainly a great hardship, what really makes a trip through this region absolutely

[32]This haunch of venison cost them only the modest sum of a quarter.

unbearable is the quality of the new settlers. They are the most villainous breed of men I have ever come across. By and large they are the scum of Ireland and America. They are crude, lazy, and inhospitable to an extreme. Nothing, nothing is more disgusting than the constant company of that sort of man. I must admit that whatever my prejudice against the Irish settlers, I always found them more hospitable and less disagreeable than the American settlers. All in all, I do not believe that such men exist anywhere in Europe.

The 17th. We left Green River rather late because Beaudoin had lingered on the Barrens, where he had turned the horses out to pasture. We set out again across the Barrens. Gradually the prospect altered; the land became less flat and yet less beautiful; the forests grew on higher land, and we found swamps in other places. We made only 22 miles that day; when a heavy rain surprised us at a shanty abominable even for this part of the world, we stopped there. Our host was a Pennsylvania German named Räcker, and his wife was an intolerable chatterbox. The bad weather collected a fairly large number of travelers in the vicinity and we were exceedingly uncomfortable. Shortly a conversation rose among the company about the distress of the western folk, and everybody railed to his heart's content. They claim to be overwhelmed by taxes, although there may be no civilized people who pay anywhere near as little. They pronounce it useless even to pay for the support of the local government of Kentucky. Everywhere they complain, with the same angry acerbity, of government by rich eastern businessmen; everywhere they parrot paltry Jacobin[33] commonplaces, that the poor work hard and the rich get richer, that the rich are not happy merely selling land at exorbitant prices but find various ways to extort what little money the settlers make, etc.

The 18th. For four or five miles more we continued through the country I have just described, the hills growing ever higher and the valleys ever deeper. After that we rode down off the plateau of the Barrens and at Mr Hodgins' place, 6 miles from Räcker's, found a fine farm, much better than any we had seen for a long time. The orchard is mature, and the trees at least seven or eight years old. Beyond Hodgins' the traveler continues sharply downhill for a long time, for the Barrens are a very high plateau. In the valleys now we began to note the renowned rich soil of Kentucky. It is truly very rich and excellent. The valley lowlands (what they call here *Bottom land*) are a black soil equal in quality to any of our good European soil. With these goodly lands we also saw thick forests again, and trees enormous in both circumference and height. In crossing the creeks we noticed that here as in the Cumberland the bed was of flat, smooth rock. At times we were even able to see the depth of the rock beneath the water, and so to see clearly the depth of the soil above the hardpan.

We had dinner in a log-house belonging to a man named Hazel,

---

33 The Duc d'Orléans is no longer the nonconformist of seventeen who joined the Club des Jacobins enthusiastically and was even appointed for a time to its presentation committee.

where we were astounded by a very tolerable meal, with fresh venison, coffee, etc.

That night we reached Beardstown[34] after considerably more downhill travel. We had a hard time finding the Bitchfork ford on the Salt river, which was in flood. We reached Beardstown after dark. There we lodged at Captain Been's. Good people and a good inn.

Beardstown is already a fairly large town for Kentucky. They say there are almost 150 houses. It is on a plateau surrounded by dense forests of tall trees. Its population is, like that of all American towns, merchants or innkeepers or laborers.

We spent two days there to bring our diaries up to date, rest our horses, and make repairs on whatever equipment had not survived so sore a trial.

May 21st. We went out of Beardstown along the Louisville road or, as they say here, the Ohio falls road. We traveled through country that seemed more thickly populated than what we had just seen. Rains some days previously had so swollen the *Salt river* that we were unable to ford it. We unloaded our horses and made them swim across, while we crossed in a canoe with all our gear. Here they give the name canoe *(canot)* to a kind of small but long boat made of a single tree trunk hollowed out by hatchet. There are such big trees in this area that large enough trunks are easy to find. All they use to

---

[34] At Bardstown on 21 May Louis-Philippe drew up his accounts. There remained $411 cash on hand, of which $197.50 was in gold and the rest in notes of $100, $50, $20, and $10, plus small change in silver.

propel them is a *pagaie*, or paddle, that is to say a short oar stroked now on one side, now on the other, which is extremely difficult if not impossible for someone not used to it. Besides, there is no keel, so at the slightest false move they capsize. They skim along very quickly and are highly efficient in upstream travel.

I return to Beardstown, having left out a brief story that may indicate how little these local folk know of the world.

An Irishman costumed as Punchinello crisscrossed the whole town on horseback, announcing a marionette show for 7 o'clock that evening. The whole town turned out, large and small; I believe people came from miles around. Beaudoin, who attended the performance, said that though it was a large hall no one could even breathe. Our host and hostess were present with their whole family, and on her return the lady told me that she was well pleased that her children had been there, because at least *in their old age* they would be able to say that they had seen it.

Louis-Philippe's diary ends abruptly on 21 May 1797, during his stay in Bardstown. At the request of his mother, the Dowager Duchesse d'Orléans, the Duc de Montpensier set down a brief memoir in 1798 of their travels after the year 1794. The passage excerpted deals with the end of the three brothers' tour of North America and Canada up to their return to Philadelphia.

119

The Duc de Montpensier's Diary

(June–November 1797)

From there they crossed a wilderness toward *Louisville* and *Lexington* in Kentucki. They relaxed for several days in *Pittsbourg*, formerly Fort *Duquesne*, famous during the time of war in *Canada*. From there they crossed another wasteland to the shores of Lakes *Erie* and *Ontario*. The expedition was arduous, exhausting, and often dangerous: they were forced to cross rivers swimming or fording, to sleep in the open almost every night often after rains all day, to eat cold food almost always, to wander in vast, trackless forests making their way by compass, with only a single servant to wait upon them and care for their horses.

M. le Duc de Montpensier survived a great danger during this trip. Having halted for a moment, he lost the trail trying to catch up with the company; he had not so much as a chunk of bread with him and it was only five or six hours later that he found his traveling companions, who had suffered cruel anxieties, as may be imagined, considering the dangers to which a wanderer is exposed when lost, without guide or supplies, in a land where the nearest dwelling may be a day or two away, and where it is all too easy to spend an eternity searching for it, when there are no landmarks or bearings amid forests bounded only by the two oceans, or impassible lakes or rivers. Such hardship was rewarded by the great impact on European travelers of their first sight of peoples still wholly savage, like the North American Indians. The princes visited several tribes of the *Six Nations*, the *Mohaks*, etc.

They crossed into *Canada* for the best view of the famous *Niagara* Falls, where the *Saint-Laurent* River, between its lakes *Erie* and *Ontario*,

Louise-Marie-Adélaïde de Bourbon, Duchesse d'Orléans, mother of Louis-Philippe, Montpensier and Beaujolais. THE NEW YORK PUBLIC LIBRARY.

cascades from a prodigious height. M. le Duc de Montpensier dashed off a sketch of it which he sent to Mme la Duchesse d'Orléans.

*L*eaving the Great Lakes behind, the wayfarers journeyed through the new settlements along the *Genessie* to see the waterfalls on the river of that name. They reached a tributary called the *Susquehanna*, down which they sailed as far as *Wilkes-Barre*, whence they returned overland to Philadelphia, at the end of July, a time when the yellow fever began its ravages in that city. There they remained until mid-September, when they departed for *New York* and *New England*. Only a few days before leaving did they learn from the public prints of the restitution of Mme la Duchesse d'Orléans' possessions. They spent three weeks in *New York*, sending thence a confidential emissary to Madame. They took ship for *Providence*, by way of *Newport*. These are the two principal cities of *Rhode Island*. The crossing by water took only thirty-some hours, though the distance is above eighty leagues. From *Providence* they traveled overland to Boston where they remained two weeks only, wanting to take advantage of the fine season to see the state of *New Hampshire* and the state of *Maine*, the northernmost of New England. They passed through *Salem, Newburyport, Portsmouth*, and *Portland*. They spent some time in those last two cities, whose populations, like those of *Boston* and *New York*, showed them every attention and interest.

The season turning chill, it was necessary to consider returning southward. Quitting Portland, the travelers retraced their steps as far as *Boston*. Being most pleased with New England and its inhabitants, they wished also to visit *Connecticut*, which is part of it. They intended to spend two weeks in *Boston* first. But the fifth or sixth day after their return to that city M. de Montpensier, scanning a newspaper, was stopped short at the sight of his mother's name. It was in an article describing the frightful catastrophe of the month of September; the newspaper offered only the barest summary, stating merely that Mme la Duchesse d'Orléans was among those deported.

This deadly blow overwhelmed her royal sons, who imagined her near death as she departed for Cayenne. From the gazette's account no other conclusion was possible. Immediately the princes left for *Philadelphia*, passing through *Connecticut* and *New York*, hoping to be met by further news in Philadelphia and to find some way to proceed to *Cayenne*, where they would effect the release of Mme la Duchesse d'Orléans, or remain to share her captivity.

The Duc de Montpensier,

Painter of the New World,

by Jean-Pierre Bukolar, curator of the Musée de l'Histoire de France

Naturally the best illustrations to accompany Louis-Philippe's American diaries are to be found among the drawings of his brother Antoine-Philippe, Duc de Montpensier; or more exactly, because he did not save his preliminary sketches, in the watercolors and paintings derived from them.

If he was not vastly talented, the prince had qualities of taste, sensitivity, and observation that were enhanced by the efficacious tutoring of Mme de Genlis. All four of Philippe-Égalité's children took lessons from the greatest artists,[1] and all four were certainly capable of reasonably adequate line drawings; Princess Adelaide even beguiled the bleak days of Swiss exile by painting small scenes or landscapes on buttons, as was then the fashion. But only Montpensier succeeded in pushing beyond naive art, childish coloring, and sentimental or pious subjects, acquiring more vigor and skill in landscape and finally, in his last lithography portraits, rather remarkable psychological insight. And Mme de Genlis had noticed his potential: "He loved the arts passionately, and above all drawing and painting, in which he excelled not merely as an amateur but as an artist. This temperament revealed itself in his childhood; and as I believe that one should cultivate all of nature's gifts, I allowed him much more time than the others for drawing" (*Mémoires* of Mme la Comtesse de Genlis, volume III).

In the next generation almost all of Louis-Philippe's children prac-

---

[1]Their art masters were Carmontelle, Bardin, David himself, and chiefly the Pole Sylvestre Myris. Cf. J. Adhémar, "L'éducation Visuelle des Fils de France," *Revue des Arts*, 6 (1956), 29–43.

ticed drawing and lithography with fair success; two among them earned recognition as genuinely inspired artists, first Princess Marie, an excellent sculptor and one of the great names among French Romantic sculptors, and then the Prince de Joinville. The latter's watercolors are well known and highly esteemed; full of charm and humor, they were painted, like true commentary, to commemorate major or minor events, or to express a pungent observation; they were to illustrate the text of his *Vieux Souvenirs*.[2]

Well before his nephew, the Duc de Montpensier had practiced such historiographic art, taking great pains to catch the fleeting event and to delineate, for quasi-pedagogical purposes, the "curiosity," be it geographic or ethnographic. This practice, already widespread in the second half of the eighteenth century and then intensified by the turbulent days of the French Revolution, would dominate much nineteenth century official art (and shortly thereafter, the illustrated press). It was to some extent encouraged by Louis-Philippe himself in his efforts to revitalize the Château de Versailles as a vast pictorial pageant of France.

So it was that while he fretted in the dank gloom of Fort Saint-Jean's dungeon in Marseilles where he at eighteen had been incarcerated with his young brother the Comte de Beaujolais, just thirteen, the Duc de Montpensier, or rather Citizen Égalité the Younger, had whiled away the days by keeping his diary and sketch-

[2]Prince de Joinville, *Vieux Souvenirs, 1818–1848* (Paris, C. Lévy, 1894). The watercolors of the War of Secession were published in Paris in 1964 with a preface by the Comte de Paris and historical notes by André Maurois and General John Gavin.

ing. He turned out little scenes in which the droll and excessively old-fashioned ways of their aged uncle the Prince de Conti, immured with them, were wickedly caricatured.[3] Only after that long imprisonment in debilitating conditions which permanently ruined their health were the two young princes permitted to join the "eldest" beyond the seas.[4] Not then overly worried about their health, Louis-Philippe immediately dragged them off on the roads and rivers of the New World, following an itinerary suggested by Washington himself. They would see great stretches of territory, and would not neglect this rich opportunity to render permanent the memorable impressions they looked forward to. All three brothers carried notebooks for travel diaries, and Montpensier was careful not to forget his portfolio and pencil.

"We shall not follow them[5] among the Cherokees, a savage nation amid whom they spent two days observing rites and celebrations, nor into the wilderness of the six nations in Canada, nor to the famous Niagara Falls, of which the Duc de Montpensier, who liked to catch views of the most spectacular spots for his album, painted a scene now hanging in the Palais-Royal with several other of his pictures.

[3] *Mémoires de S. A. S. Antoine-Philippe d'Orléans, Duc de Montpensier, Prince du Sang* (Paris, Baudouin Frères, 1824). The watercolors are there reproduced by lithography.

[4] All three had their portraits done in New York in 1797, in pastels, by the American painter James Sharpless. Only the portrait of Louis-Philippe is extant; it was offered for sale at Sotheby's in 1974.

[5] An introductory note (doubtless by J. Vatout) to the *Mémoires* of the Duc de Montpensier, *op. cit.*

The three brothers stood up well under the strain of that long, arduous journey through uninhabited regions; they were young and united after long sufferings; they were traveling together and unhindered in a new world fascinating to Europeans: what pleasures were scattered among their hardships!" And we read further: "Beneath these fresh skies the three brothers never separated: during the long journeys they undertook together, the Duc de Montpensier eagerly filled his portfolio with most remarkable sketches of vivid scenery. He did a version of Niagara Falls, to be seen among several others of his composition in the gallery at the Palais Royal, notably his conversation with his brother Beaujolais in their cell in the tower of Fort Saint-Jean in Marseilles."[6]

In his diaries Louis-Philippe twice mentions his brother's drawings: "We stopped for a look at Cecil Furnace, below a waterfall on Cecil Creek of which Montpensier made a sketch," and "The artificial hill from which we first saw Tôkona was made in that way . . . and it was from there that Montpensier sketched the village." A third sketch is of a spot described in the diaries, the Little Falls of the Potomac (4 April 1797).

Unfortunately we no longer have Montpensier's preliminary sketches.[7] They were intended to supply detail for his landscape

[6]Life of Montpensier (probably by Vatout, excerpted from *Biographie des Contemporains*), published following his *Mémoires, op. cit.*

[7]Was this the portfolio of drawings that Louis-Philippe showed to the American painter George Catlin in 1845? Cf. John Francis MacDermott, "French Pictorial Reporters of the American Scene," in *France and North America: Over Three Hundred Years of Dialogue* (Lafayette,

compositions, in which no doubt strict topographical precision had to be sacrificed to the inner meaning of a natural scene (the falls) or a human setting (the Indian village of Tokono). These creations were first watercolors, painted after the return to Philadelphia; at least one of them was, if we may believe Montpensier's letter to his sister Adelaide after his visit to Niagara Falls, in that latter part of their journey unfortunately omitted from Louis-Philippe's diaries:[8] "It is the most impressive, the most majestic sight that I have ever seen; its height is 137 feet and the volume of water is immense, being the whole St. Lawrence River cascading over the one spot; I did a sketch of it and am planning to do a watercolor that my darling little sister will surely see at our devoted mother's; but I have not yet begun it, and it will take me some time, for it is truly not a small piece of work." That watercolor was indeed painted and sent to the Duchesse d'Orléans, exiled in Spain.[9] It can be identified, seemingly, as one of the four watercolors belonging to Mgr le Comte de Paris; identically framed, all four are doubtless Montpensier's work—his monogram can barely be deciphered on one of them—and are therefore repro-

Louisiana, 1973). In Louis-Philippe's notebooks there is a rather formless landscape in crayon. Some coarse and vulgar murals at the Talbot Tavern in Bardstown (Kentucky), where indeed the princes stopped from 18 to 21 May 1797, are also attributed to him, without the slightest evidence.

[8]"Later dated Philadelphia, 14 August 1797, published in J. Vatout, *Notices Historiques sur les Tableaux de la Galerie de S. A. R. Mgr le Duc d'Orléans* (Paris, 1826), IV, 27.

[9]"M. le Duc de Montpensier did a sketch of this from which he later made a picture which he sent to Madame la Duchesse d'Orléans." (Hand-written memoir of Montpensier's travels.)

duced here. Aside from Niagara, they depict a waterfall (Cecil Creek? above the Susquehanna), the Little Falls of the Potomac, and the site of Swancks Bridge.

When the three brothers took up residence in England in 1800, Montpensier could familiarize himself with new techniques by consorting with London artists like Cosway and Lawrence, and seeking their advice. So he tried oil painting, did portraits which he sold to his friends, and reworked his American landscapes as oils: in 1804 the *View of Tokono* and *Niagara*, and in 1805 a composition on the great river he sailed down in January 1798, *Souvenir du Mississippi*.[10] He offered the *View of Tokono* to the Duke of Kent (later father of the future Queen Victoria) and *Souvenir du Mississippi* to Queen Charlotte of England. Nothing is now known of those canvases, while the third, the *View of Niagara*, signed and dated 1804, was in Louis-Philippe's collections in the Palais-Royal until 1848 and hangs today in the Museum of the New-York Historical Society, which has kindly authorized its reproduction here.[11]

In truth the prince had been trained chiefly as a draftsman. During his excursions to the castles and country houses of English high

---

[10]"The scene is imaginary, or rather, as he himself said, it is a memory of the river's character and the landscapes along its banks" (Vatout, *Notices Historiques* . . . IV, 529). In a private collection we saw a pastel signed by Montpensier and dated 1805, entitled *Souvenir du Mississippi*.

[11]"The space between the two falls in nature has been reduced in the painting so that they can be combined in one point of view." Cf. Vatout, *Notices Historiques* . . . , IV, 517. The point of view is shifted ninety degrees from that of the watercolor. The canvas was hung in the Museum of the New-York Historical Society in 1950.

View of Niagara Falls, which the princes visited 21 June 1797. Painting by Montpensier (1804). MUSEUM OF THE NEW-YORK HISTORICAL SOCIETY.

society, he turned out a profusion of much appreciated pencil drawings, which the future King Charles X of France characterized as "pretty drawings of romantic sites." He then learned that a recently invented process would permit reproduction of his drawings in several copies: namely, lithography. Developed in 1796 by the Bavarian Aloys Senefelder, it had not yet been applied to the reproduction of works of art. Senefelder visited London in 1800–1801. Whether Montpensier met him, or learned indirectly of the process, which Senefelder registered with the British Patent Office in 1800, we do not know. We do know that he was one of the first artists, if not the first, to use it to reproduce drawings. His first lithographs, signed *A. P. D'O fecit* (Antoine-Philippe d'Orléans), are indeed dated 1804, the Year One of lithography; the others bear the dates 1805 and 1806. These priceless incunabula of the new art depict castles in England and Wales drawn in a rather soft line, and excellent portraits of the three brothers d'Orléans[12] and of a young woman, perhaps Lady Charlotte Rawdon, whom Montpensier dreamed of marrying. But his health was already declining. Ravaged by tuberculosis, he died 18 May 1807.

Louis-Philippe, when he settled in Palermo after his marriage to Maria Amelia of the Two Sicilies, sent for his brother's works and had them set in order by an émigré, M. de Joinville, an amateur

---

[12]In a letter of 14 January 1806 Montpensier announces to his sister the dispatch of "a second edition of my portrait and also our elder brother's, done by me by the same method as the others, that is, on stone." Shortly before, he had told her, "Everybody thinks these profiles excellent likenesses."

137

painter. "Uncrated poor Montpensier's beautiful pictures, just arrived from England," Maria Amelia wrote in her diary 7 November 1810. Once back in France, the Duc d'Orléans had them hung in his picture gallery in the Palais-Royal. Following the advice of his librarian J. Vatout, he decided to use them as the basis of an historiographical series narrating the episodes of their adventurous youth. They drew up a preliminary list of paintings to be commissioned, which list we still have. Concerning the United States we may note: The America; Philadelphia—the brothers—Marc South; At Washington's; Cherakis—savages; Niagara; At Pitzbourg; On the Mississippi; The frigate Cochrane (Thetis). . . . On a second list, crosses mark the commissions actually confirmed: The Vessel America (X); Arrival in Philadelphia (1796); Reunion with His Brothers (1797) (X); Mount Vernon, Washington's Home (X); Among the Cherakis (the blood-letting) (X); Niagara; Return to Boston—sketch of Dauberval; New York; An Excursion in Maine or Massachusetts; On the Mississippi; New Orleans; Captain Cochrane's Frigate. . . .

Certain of the commissioned paintings were based closely on originals by Montpensier. So the painter Storelli[13] did a *Souvenir du Mississippi* in 1816 and a *View of Tokono* in 1819; the painter Ronmy[14]

[13]Felice Maria Fernando Storelli (1778–1854). Cf. J. Vatout, *Notices Historiques* . . . IV, 529, 531. "The scene, done from memory, is inexact; but it resembles the site of Tokono and gives some idea of savage settlements. This one is inhabited by Cherokees."

[14]Guillaume Frédéric Ronmy (1786–1854). Cf. J. Vatout, *Notices Historiques* . . . , IV, 527–28. In Montpensier's hand-written memoir of his travels we read the following: "Leaving the Great Lakes behind, the wayfarers journeyed through the new settlements along the *Genessie* to see the waterfalls on the river of that name. They reached a tributary of the river called

138

View of the upper falls of the Genesee, near Lake Ontario (Rochester, New York), where the Seneca Indians live. This is probably the painting commissioned by Louis-Philippe from the painter Romny (1823) and inspired by a lost gouache of Montpensier. At the left are the three princes, their servant Beaudoin and the American Jhos Morris.

MUSEUM OF THE NEW-YORK HISTORICAL SOCIETY.

a *View of the Upper Falls of the Genesee* in 1823 and another of *The Natural Bridge at Rockbridge in Virginia;* and the painter Bidauld[15] a *View of the Three Princes d'Orléans before Niagara Falls*. Of them all we know today only the *View of the Genesee* hanging in the Museum of the New-York Historical Society and reproduced here with the Museum's kind permission. Finally, Louis-Philippe had certain of the pictures in his gallery reproduced in a sumptuous collection of lithographs.[16] He thus ensured his brother's works a distribution that the latter could never have dared hope for. So it is through these lithographs that we know the invaluable *View of Tokono*, by which the Duc de Montpensier, like any good ethnologist, hoped to pass along to us accurate visual testimony of what he saw among the Cherokee Indians.

---

[15] Joseph Bidauld (1758–1846). The picture was painted for Mme Adélaïde, who made a gift of it to her son. Cf. J. Vatout, *Notices Historiques* . . . , IV, 9.

[16] *Galerie Lithographiée de S. A. R. Mgr le Duc d'Orléans*, 2 vols. (Paris, n.d.). The works reproduced are the views of Niagara and Tokona. We may compare Montpensier's works to a series of French lithographs on *"North America"* adapted around 1825 from drawings by Jacques Milbert (1766–1840), with French or English captions. We may also mention the precious pictures by the Chevalier Alex. Lesueur of his travels in America (1816–37), now in the Museum of Natural History in Le Havre.

the *Susquehanna,* down which they sailed as far as *Wilkes-Barre,* whence they returned overland to Philadelphia at the end of July." *The View of the Genesee* was acquired by the Museum of the New-York Historical Society in 1867 (formerly in the Bryan collection). The princes were at the Genesee 12 July 1797.

View of the Hudson River from Tappan Bay, New York. Oil on canvas by Robert Havell (1793–1898). MUSEUM OF THE NEW-YORK HISTORICAL SOCIETY.

Afterword

by Suzanne d'Huart,
curator of the Archives
de la Maison de France

"Having wandered about Europe for three and a half years, with never a certain income and no refuge save among strangers, I left for America 24 September 1796, at my mother's request."

Briefly summarizing that episode of his life, Louis-Philippe explains in his *Memoirs* the reasons for his departure, a new adventure after so many others. He had left France 15 April 1793 to begin an exile that would keep him far from his homeland for twenty-two long years. "My story since my departure of France is a romance...."†

After service in the armies of the Republic, after distinguishing himself at Valmy and Jemappes, the time came when it was wiser for him to leave France and live incognito. At the college in Reichenau, Switzerland, he taught mathematics, geography, and languages under the name of "Chabos." He lived in Hamburg as "M. Ludovic." Scandinavia received the visit of a "M. Müller," who traveled through Denmark, Sweden, Norway, and Finland, also visiting Lapland, where he roamed for three weeks, most often on foot, camping with the Lapps, living like them on milk and reindeer meat.

His was an endless struggle for security and subsistence, for letters of credit, for some way out of a particularly tangled financial situation. It was out of the question to count on revenues from France, where, if not for the Revolution, he would have found himself the richest man in the kingdom. He had brought away with him only the equivalent of £800 sterling, in cash and other assets, but was able to

---

† In English in the original.

lay his hands on more money afterward, thanks to businessmen of various nationalities. A banker of Antwerp, Walter Boyd, held in trust a sum raised on the patrimonial property of Avesnes, and he had firm instructions from Philippe-Égalité† to remit it either to Philippe-Égalité himself or, "in case of trouble," to his children. The sale of diamonds entrusted by their father to the Dutch banker Walckiers would also contribute indirectly to an improvement in the young princes' situation.‡

Thomas Coutts, the kind, devoted, and faithful London banker of the House of Orléans, made remittances through the intermediary of Magistrate Hottinguer and bankers and businessmen of Zurich, Berne, and Hamburg.

At the beginning of 1796, just back in Hamburg from his trip to the far north, the young Duc d'Orléans was weary and discouraged, despite his strength of character. Although he was pleased that his sister Adelaide had found refuge with her aunt, the Princesse de Conti, he was on the other hand extremely upset about his mother and his two brothers. He knew how precarious was the position of the Duchesse d'Orléans, still in France, whose father's popularity had kept her from harm. But the good and charitable Duc de Penthièvre

---

†Louis-Philippe's father, a liberal nobleman of royal blood who became "Citoyen Égalité" and voted for the death of his cousin Louis XVI but was nevertheless guillotined in the Reign of Terror.

‡In France, a prince was any son of the royal house, however tenuous and cousinly his prospects of succession. (Princes vary with countries. In England the title is reserved to sons and grandsons of a monarch. In Russia it implied descent from one or another dynasty, and all male members of the family might use it; it became little more than a courtesy title.)

had not survived his grief at the atrocious death of his daughter-in-law, the Princesse de Lamballe; he died 4 March 1793. The duchess, after detention in a Luxembourg prison, had sought asylum in an exclusive nursing home, one of the few sanctuaries—expensive—from the Revolutionary Tribunal and the scaffold. There she lived, extremely anxious over her own fate and that of her sons Montpensier and Beaujolais. Despite their youth—they were eighteen and thirteen—they had not been spared by the decrees that fell upon the princes of the House of Bourbon, and, locked up in Fort Saint-Jean in Marseilles, there endured an arduous captivity.

Their mother's constant tears, wails, and sighs had, happily, inspired one of her companions in the nursing home. His name was Rouzel, a former member of the National Convention, and he used his influence with the Directory. A compact was concluded. The two young prisoners in Marseilles would be set free, on the express condition that their elder brother embark for America. To be absolutely certain of this prince's departure—his consequence and possible political ambitions posed dangers—a representative of the Republic would witness and certify his embarkation. His brothers would then follow him, and their mother could remain in Paris, which was her dearest wish. In May of 1796 she addressed an urgent letter to her eldest son: "The country's interest and that of your own flesh and blood ask this sacrifice of you: that you place the barrier of the seas between us."

To that entreaty, which he received 15 August, the Duc d'Orléans answered the same day: "When my beloved mother receives this letter, her orders will have been executed, and I shall be on my way to America." Would he not be making an old dream come true, taking the course he had urged upon his father in 1792, which would so greatly have altered the family's destiny? The year before, he himself had seriously considered going to the New World, where an interesting situation had been proposed to him. The time had come to put his plans into effect.

By 1796, twenty years after independence, the young American republic had already welcomed numerous Frenchmen, like Chateaubriand, Talleyrand, Volney, and so many others. The three young princes, forbidden to set foot in their own country, might find on this new and—they were sure—rapidly developing continent a temporary refuge, and perhaps even permanent asylum.

Timely financial help facilitated the organization of their trip. Gouverneur Morris, former American Minister in France, a rich American who had been one of those often in the Duchesse d'Orléans' company at the Palais-Royal during the early years of the French Revolutionary government and had remained attached to her, had learned of the bankruptcy of Edouard Walckiers, the banker who until then had supplied funds to the Duc d'Orléans. On 17 July 1796 Morris established credit with a broker in Hamburg. Louis-Philippe was thus enabled to repay what he owed Walckiers, forward money to his sister, and use the remaining funds for his journey to America.

He embarked from Hamburg on the *America* with his groom Beaudoin, and that handsome, copper-sheathed vessel sailed 24 September 1796. After an uncomfortable but uneventful crossing of

only twenty-seven days, the Duc d'Orléans debarked at Philadelphia, which was then the largest city in the United States.

There he spent four months alone, well received by local notables and by compatriots exiled like himself, and enjoying a tender and short-lived idyll with the charming Abby Willing, sister-in-law of the rich businessman Bingham.

Impatiently he awaited his two brothers, who had embarked 5 November 1796 at Marseilles aboard a Swedish ship, the *Jupiter*, not appearing under their own names on the ship's papers or the bill of health. The crew and passengers were all Americans ransomed from Algeria, where they had been held in slavery, and the princes had replaced two of them who had decided at the last moment not to go.

Montpensier and Beaujolais, already debilitated by long confinement—forty-three months—had to fight to survive, so exhausted were they by storms, bad food, lack of fresh food, and the promiscuity on board.

Finally on 6 February 1797, after a harrowing voyage of ninety-three days, they set foot "on that land so longed for" where they were joyfully united with their elder brother, whom they had not seen for three years. He himself was overwhelmed with pity for these gaunt, fair young men with emaciated faces. "But the happy reunion with my brothers in Philadelphia only added their burdens to my own." Until now he had surmounted many obstacles, and thanks to his indomitable courage, his incisive character, and the help of his devoted friends, he had been able to stay alive, improve himself, travel. There was no question now of going incognito. These exiles approached the New World under the names "Messieurs d'Orléans."

Why lead an artificial life in Philadelphia's high society, where conversation turned almost solely on money and how to make it, when they had only slender resources and were beyond the age of illusions? They knew they must give up any immediate idea of making a fortune in this country, live conservatively, and see what happened.

These two young men were twenty-two and seventeen, and their elder brother now became their mentor at twenty-three; what should he do with them? He had left them still adolescent, and the interval had not taught them the gravity and seriousness which had become the marks of his own character, formed by troubles and hardships. He was afraid that they would misuse the idleness which hung so heavily upon him, and allow themselves to be seduced into pleasures and dissipations. A long expedition would be a perfect outlet: it would keep them busy, shape them, educate them, and introduce them to a country vastly different from those of Europe. Spring was coming, the best time to begin a journey.

Exile would offer them the chance to wander the backwoods of these lands, study unknown manners and customs, explore beautiful landscapes, dazzle themselves with memorable sights, live one of the most cherished dreams of their contemporaries. After the accounts of early travelers, the War of Independence and La Fayette's popularity had roused great interest in this new continent, and in the political and social evolution of the young democracy.

Its romantic ideals had inspired several important works of litera-

View of Niagara Falls. Gouache probably painted by Montpensier and sent by him to his mother (collection of the Comte de Paris). PHOTO, FLAMMARION.

ture. In 1791, on the advice of Malesherbes, Chateaubriand set out for America, with extensive plans for exploration. He never completed them. But the "exotic" magnificence of the New World struck a chord much more personal in him than in professional explorers. So in essence the account he later published would not be a travel diary. In counterpoint to his *Journey in America* later inserted into the *Mémoires d'Outre-Tombe*, his romantic works—*Atala, The Natchez*—are of the same stock as *Paul et Virginie*. And do we not note a foreshadowing of this American "romanticism" in the tragic death of Manon Lescaut?

How would these three young princes, their spirits nourished by travel diaries and the novels of Rousseau and Bernardin de Saint-Pierre, respond to the New World?

Before striking out into the wilderness, they first were obliged to organize the physical details of their tour.

Montpensier and Beaujolais had brought along an amount estimated later, in the final accounts, at 3,056 piastres. On 24 March their brother went to the bank to withdraw $200 in gold and $1,000 in bills, drawing on transfers by agents of Coutts, the banker in London, as well as Westphalen, the Hamburg broker who had come to the young Duc d'Orléans' aid at his departure.

The purchase of four horses, which would be their primary means of locomotion, came to $930, and the tack $70.

With $1,218.50† in their purse, the three brothers, their faithful

---

†The $200 left after purchase of horses and tack, plus the piastres exchanged at three to a dollar.

Beaudoin riding behind, left Philadelphia at noon, 25 March 1797. Wearing buckskin breeches, boots, and woollen cloaks, they carried in their saddlebags, aside from blankets and oilskins, letters of recommendation, maps, and a compass to keep them to the route suggested. Crossing Maryland, Virginia, the Alleghenies, Tennessee, the Cherokee Indian territories, and Kentucky; passing along the Ohio River, Pittsburgh, the Great Lakes, and Canada and returning to Philadelphia via the northern regions, they would see rapidly growing cities like Baltimore and the new capital, Washington, as well as vast, uninhabited stretches and huge forests; they would also come to know recent emigrants of all nationalities who were seeking their fortune with better or worse luck. They would meet Indians too, the first inhabitants of this land.

Before setting out, Louis-Philippe carefully included two small notebooks of thick paper in his baggage, to keep his travel diary. That habit had earlier been drummed into him by his famous governess, Mme de Genlis, when, just before the Revolution, she took him to Spa and La Trappe. In the fashion of the time, she had taught him to set down his travel impressions, to note itineraries, describe landscapes, recount anecdotes, list expenses; and he had not forgotten her teachings, as indeed he forgot nothing of his thorough and strict education.

At various of their stops the three brothers applied themselves to their inkwells, filling page after page with memories of the day's events. Montpensier's and Beaujolais' notebooks have disappeared. But Louis-Philippe's two small notebooks have come down to us, bound in cardboard, covered in marbled pink and green paper, comprising 203 pages in a large meticulous hand. Louis-Philippe, who was all his life as wordy in conversation as in his letters and his writings, intersperses among his many fascinating notes long digressions on landscapes that had impressed him and certain particularly striking episodes. Passages crossed out, or underlined, and later corrections testify to his precision and attention to detail. And as with so many eighteenth-century voyagers, it is indeed his details, his precision, which stand out, in this travel diary. The young duke's experiences were forging and tempering him to be future king of France. So here it is faithful observation that counts, and not the more intimate chords struck by writers attuned to exoticism; yet for all that we do not lack the picturesque, or vivacity of personal reaction.

The account begins on the very day of departure, 25 March 1797, but is interrupted 21 May at Bardstown. The Duc d'Orléans, ill, forsook his diary and so merely entered the expenses of the trip's last weeks, which brought them back to Philadelphia 26 July. They could then rest after an arduous expedition, during which they had fought constantly to assure themselves decent food and lodgings. Only two visits—one to General Washington's home at Mount Vernon from 5 to 8 April, when they had the joy of receiving a first letter from their mother, and one to Asylum in Pennsylvania on 21 June—had been truly restful stops. In Asylum, a colony founded by French émigrés, they were grateful for real comfort, and for their hosts' courtesy in organizing a *fête champêtre* in their honor. Here was high society again, refinement, the pleasures and comforts of the good life, and also no doubt the sort of food their palates were accustomed to. Before going on their way they were able to stock up on eight dollars worth of provisions.

On the road good inns had been few and far between. How many times had they been forced to settle for a night in the common room of a decrepit shack, in pairs on ragged pallets, or simply stretched out on a floor made of uneven logs! Astonished by the rusticity of the houses of *"Messieurs les Newsettlers américains,"* they were also scandalized by blatant promiscuity, not to mention other indecent sights offered to their amazed eyes.

Toward the end of the journey, the need to economize their dwindling resources often forced them to bivouac in the woods, wrapped in their cloaks and blankets, sometimes soaked to the bone and devoured by mosquitoes; or even to sleep beneath the stars, as they did 2 July on the beaches of Lake Erie.

If only they had been able to fill their bellies! But rarely could they truly take the edge off their hunger and satisfy appetites sharpened by the open air and the hardship of their long rides through dense forest and over rough roads. To their constant despair, the inns usually offered—after a very long wait—mediocre food: cornbread and fried bacon, sometimes salt beef, bad coffee. A plate of hot meat or venison was the rarest of events. Their horses suffered equally and at the end of their journey were so exhausted that the three brothers and their servant had to cover the last hundred leagues in part by water, in part on foot or in hired hacks, finally returning to Philadelphia by public coach.

And actually, what were they to the colonists and innkeepers they met on this ramble, planned for five weeks but lasting four whole months and covering almost three thousand miles? Down-at-heels tourists, and suspicious characters. What were they doing here? Their simple dress and crude gear showed that they were not speculators or businessmen prospecting for land purchases or business enterprises. It was often difficult to see them for what they were: men of simple curiosity eager to admire nature, to explore the New World, to learn new things and observe folkways and customs. Their "philosophy" roused admiration among some of their hosts (here where money was king), who were quite astonished to learn that the princes' financial troubles did not diminish their courage or good humor.

Although their youthful enthusiasm in this journey was often dampened, the three brothers had some good times too, notably at the village of Tellico, where Louis-Philippe smoked pipes with the Indians and admired their tomahawks and where, as always intrigued by foreign languages, he allowed himself the pleasure of learning something of the Cherokee dialect. He showed a lively interest in their tribal ways but, raised to respect the opposite sex, was quite shocked to note that in this remote land where people lived by the laws of nature, the men assigned all hard work to their women, reserving to themselves the nobler tasks and spending the better part of the day smoking and gossiping. And yet these most hospitable "savages" often struck the princes as "the best people in the world." "Our being French was a major reason for their hospitality, as they love our nation infinitely," Montpensier wrote to his sister Adelaide 14 August 1797, after reporting his awe at the grandiose spectacle of Niagara Falls.

Like all tourists, the three brothers brought back a few souvenirs of the lands they had visited: Indian pipes, belts, saddles, a bearskin, tobacco pouches. But for those as for everything, costs had to be managed carefully. There were so many expenses: the faithful Beau-

162

View of Swancks Bridge. Gouache by Montpensier. His monogram is discernible at the lower right (collection of the Comte de Paris).

PHOTO, FLAMMARION.

doin's wages; the score at inns, often as exorbitant at the bad ones as at the good ones; corn and oats and shoes for the horses; tolls at ferries and bridges; the replacement of worn clothes and boots; laundry, a problem at each stop; postage fees, very high in those remote regions; whiskey and rum, which Montpensier and Beaujolais were very fond of and which their elder brother finally purchased for them, seeing the strength ebb in their gaunt bodies. How could they be calm and cheerful amid constant expense and a shrinking purse! Of the $1,200 they began with, only $411 remained by 21 May.

On his return to Philadelphia Louis-Philippe must have come into some money, undoubtedly forwarded by his European bankers, since he led his brothers off on another trip, this one to Maine by way of New York, Providence, and Boston. At Pittsburgh on 18 June the travelers had joyfully received a thick packet of letters bringing news at last of their mother and sister. Their hopes rose again when they learned that a decree had finally restored their mother's possessions. Their financial situation might improve and, failing a return to France, which they did not then foresee, settling in an eastern American city might be a solution. Their London banker, Thomas Coutts, who corresponded regularly with Louis-Philippe, offered the sincere hope that their luck would turn brighter as matters improved. "In a gloomy and adverse sky, friends and swallows are seldom to be found."†

But the Directory blocked the decree, and the Duchesse d'Orléans

† In English in the original.

had to leave France and proceed to Spain, while her possessions, so far merely sequestered, were now confiscated and put up for sale as national assets.

When they heard, in Boston, that their mother had been deported, the three sons knew only one resolve, to join her in her exile. On 10 December they set out once more across America. With the usual multitude of problems, they sailed down the Ohio and the Mississippi and arrived in New Orleans on 12 February 1798, where they were received with the honors due to descendants of the Regent.†

Their purse was full, thanks to large loans. In August and November 1797 Gouverneur Morris had sent them $4,000, which swelled the sum lent them by Richard Gernon in August. In New Orleans a rich citizen, Bernard de Marigny, pressed a loan upon them in token of his own French origins.

So by 17 February the three brothers boarded an American ship bound for Havana, where, in their capacity as princes "of the same blood as Philip V," they received a splendid welcome. On the very day of their arrival an extremely rich old lady, Doña Leonor de Contreras, placed a magnificent grandly furnished house at their disposal, complete with servants and carriages. Happy as they were to return to a way of life so different from their many months of hardship, they fretted at being delayed in Havana for eighteen months. But once more they adapted themselves to the manners and customs of a new country: they wore their hair long, hanging, and

† Their great-great-grandfather, the second Duc d'Orléans, had served as Regent when Louis XV succeeded at the age of five.

166

Detail of view of the upper falls of the Genesee (plate 22). The three princes, Beaudoin and Jhos Morris. MUSEUM OF THE NEW-YORK HISTORICAL SOCIETY.

powdered, and at sunset they took the air along public promenades in *volantes*, one-horse cabriolets driven by a Negro. Of course they learned Spanish, still intending to rejoin their mother. But instead of that impatiently awaited authorization from the Court of Spain, they received a brutal order of expulsion, which was relayed by the Captain General of the island of Cuba in September 1799. They had to leave Havana immediately. And so it was that in the great returning wave of European exiles, Louis-Philippe and his brothers landed in England in January of 1800, after an improbable voyage, dictated by circumstances, that took them to the Bahamas, Halifax, and New York.

But the Duc d'Orléans' wanderings were not at an end; nor were his money troubles, despite his "allowance" from the British government and his marriage to Maria Amelia of Sicily.

On 22 May 1810 he departed Palermo for Spain to renew an effort begun in 1808 to establish himself there or in South America. His sadness at leaving his "most dear" wife was intensified by his anxieties, which he shared with Maria Amelia in a memorandum on the state of their common finances. He reminded her of the pensions due his mother, his sister, and his faithful companions and servants, and also to take care of his "American debts." He had been able to repay Richard Gernon in 1809 thanks to the sale of horses left behind in Philadelphia, but with his customary precision he enumerated the settlements pending: the $4,000 due "Mr Gouverneur Morris of New York, who has a wooden leg and was Minister in France where he was very close to the late King Louis XVI and my mother," the sum due M. de Marigny of New Orleans, and finally the sum due the heirs of Don Gabriel d'Aristizabal, lieutenant general of the Spanish navy and commandant in Havana. He also mentioned the $8,000 due Doña Leonor de Contreras, but indicated that their generous hostess expected repayment no more than Havana's nobility, who had raised money to help them return to Europe.

Bernard de Marigny's loan was repaid in 1813, with receipt and without complications. Gouverneur Morris, while he had been a faithful friend in need, was first and foremost a careful businessman, and the matter was less simple. In 1812 the former American Minister, who had retired to his estate at Morrisania in New York, learned from the newspapers that his old debtor was receiving funds from the British treasury. He immediately set about recovering his money through intermediaries. But Morris specified clearly that it was no longer merely a matter of the $4,000 lent so long ago: from 1797 to 1802, he claimed, money had been so tight that the normal interest rate was 3 percent per month. The money, both the principal and the interest, was eventually repaid.

Among all of Louis-Philippe's youthful memories, his American wayfaring was what he most enjoyed recalling. He never neglected an opportunity to mention some feature of it or to tell a story, especially when, with his customary courtesy and warmth, he gave audience to American citizens passing through Paris.

On 13 July 1842, Louis-Philippe's eldest son fractured his skull in a bad fall at an elegant Neuilly grocery shop, and the king and queen attended him there as he lay dying. In that highly dramatic setting

Louis-Philippe tried to console the queen, distraught with grief, by recalling an incident from that distant past. "I took a similar fall in America, and was unconscious for three hours." To ease their long and tragic vigil he must have told her once again how, after regaining consciousness, he bled himself before the residents of Carlisle, who were amazed at his knowledge and skill. He was still hoping against hope that his unfortunate son would be restored by meaningless treatments: cupping, leeches, mustard plasters, and repeated bleedings started by an enamel penknife, the blade of which still bears traces of the princely blood.

Early in his exile at Claremont after the revolution of 1848, the king requested that certain documents be located and sent on to him. He made special mention of his American notebooks. They were testimony to the great adventure of his youth, when he explored a new, free land, and enjoyed enlightened politics, fruitful contacts, and precious friendships.

The tradition which Louis-Philippe had established was maintained after him. The Prince de Joinville made two trips through Canada and the United States, taking with him his son, the Duc de Penthièvre. At the beginning of the American Civil War he served as observer and adviser in the Army of the Potomac, where Louis-Philippe's two grandsons, the Comte de Paris and the Duc de Chartres, were serving as officers under the command of General McClellan. Like his grandfather before him at the same age, the Comte de Paris kept up his "daily journal" in 1862. In neat handwriting and with the same attention to detail he sets down his routes, describes his trips, passes judgment on the soldiers and civilians he met, and rejoices in the warm welcome given him everywhere.

Louis-Philippe's American notebooks, deposited in the National Archives in 1969 and 1970, are the property of the Fondation Saint-Louis, curators of the Archives of the House of France. Monseigneur the Comte de Paris has very kindly authorized publication of the full text according to the original manuscript.

174

1815: A Memoir by Louis-Philippe on Napoleon's Hundred Days

*L*ouis-Philippe seemed fated to exile. Three times more—twice in 1815!—he would have to leave his country.

In France the Revolutionary era became the Napoleonic, and its spirit as well as its armies swept over Europe. But after the military disasters of 1812 and 1813, Napoleon's empire lay in ruins. He fought on inside France, but in April of 1814 was deposed, and late that month sailed to exile on Elba.

Louis XVIII was restored to the throne. He was a grandson, in the Dauphin's line, of Louis XV, and a younger brother of the guillotined Louis XVI; he was also Louis-Philippe's cousin. With the throne he acquired Europe's most brilliant (and once most fervent) army, led by a corps of marshals and generals never equaled and now legendary, many of whom figure in this account. Their allegiance was ultimately to France and not to any man, and as long as Louis XVIII reigned unchallenged, most served him well and faithfully.

But on March 1, 1815, Napoleon landed in southern France, and his astonishing Hundred Days began. Once more France was wracked by war and divided loyalties.

Louis-Philippe gives us a memoir from the royalist side. His sensibility is notably more aristocratic now, and his style more pompous and involute, but he retains much of his youthful good sense. And he has not forgotten the most important lesson of his exile in America: the superiority of constitutional government over despotism.

S.B.

5 March –
25 March 1815

A catastrophe as grim as it is unexpected has just stunned all Europe. A king loved and trusted by his people has been driven from his own capital and his realm overrun soon afterward by the man whose very name evokes calamities and crimes; and from the state of peace and prosperity to which it had been restored, France has been plunged once again, in less than three weeks, into the chasm of evil and disorder it had believed forever sealed. It is important to set forth the inexorable chain of events by which treason, at this grave juncture, paralyzed the military establishment and the national will.

On March 5th the king learned by semaphore that Bonaparte had landed on French soil at the head of eleven hundred men. That bold stroke could be interpreted in two ways: it was either the climax of a plot promoted by an extensive conspiracy, or the act of a madman whose ambition, and the violence of whose nature, had rendered intolerable a peace which condemned him to a turmoil of remorse. In either case it was necessary to take measures which common prudence suggested and which clear and present danger prescribed. Troops were ordered to muster with all urgency at Lyon. Optimistic reports were received from the commandant at Grenoble, and the conduct of the garrison in Antibes gave reason to hope that Bonaparte was wrong if he hoped to rally the king's troops to his cause. Should he nevertheless have formed some alliances, units stationed in Lyon were to check him. *Monsieur*† left on the morning of the 6th

<hr>

†The Comte d'Artois, younger brother of Louis XVIII, whom he succeeded in 1824 as Charles X.

to take command of those units, and was followed next day by M. le Duc d'Orléans.†

All marshals and generals stationed in the provinces were ordered to assume their respective commands. Marshal Ney, who commanded at Besançon and could there provide tactical support for *Monsieur*, came to take his leave of the king. In kissing His Majesty's hand, he announced in tones of devotion, and apparently in a spirit of bluff soldier's honesty, that if he caught up with the enemy of the king and of France "he would bring him back in an iron cage." Events proved that he was even then lying ignobly, inspired by the prospect of a betrayal that every military man in Europe would learn of with horror.

Monsieur was greeted enthusiastically at Lyon. All was made ready for the most determined resistance, but unfortunately no munitions were available.

Soon it was learned that the garrison at Grenoble had opened the city gates, and that one regiment, under the command of M. de la Bédoyère, had gone over to the rebels. Only a small number of troops had by then arrived in Lyon; but *Monsieur*, whom Marshal Macdonald‡ had rushed to reinforce, decided for all that to hold fast behind hastily erected barricades. Upon the appearance of the first dragoons in Bonaparte's vanguard, however, desertion became gen-

---

† As Louis-Philippe refers to himself throughout.
‡ Also called the Duc de Tarente (Taranto).

180

eral among *Monsieur's* troops. All the Duc de Tarente's remonstrances were in vain, and then, as since, forces mobilized to resist the tide only swelled it and augmented its violence.

We learned on the 10th, by semaphore and therefore without details, that Bonaparte had entered Lyon that same day. M. le Duc d'Orléans returned to Paris on the 12th. *Monsieur* arrived there the next day. Subsequent reports portended a rapid succession of disasters.

Meanwhile rumor, excited by so many fears and suspicions, sought the causes of his deplorable success elsewhere than in the energy and authority of the man himself. No one wanted to believe that his personal magnetism had produced such an effect on the troops. Marshal the Duc de Dalmatie,[†] Minister of War, had been the last to abandon Napoleon's lost cause, fighting to the end. Many now interpreted his earlier display of devotion to duty as a mark of treason. There was no slightest evidence of such treason, and it should perhaps be counted among the innumerable popular slanders that circulate at moments of great peril; but public opinion blazed out against the Marshal, and he personally placed his resignation and his épée in the king's hands. His Majesty, with the confidence that never deserted him even amid the most craven betrayals, called upon the Duc de Feltre,[‡] whom general sentiment recommended to his choice, and invested him with the war ministry he had held under Bonaparte

[†]That is, Dalmatia. This was Marshal Soult.

[‡]Marshal Clarke.

until the Restoration. The king's confidence was amply justified by the Duc de Feltre's loyalty.

The only reasonable course now was to pull back the troops; almost everywhere, to send them out against the enemy was to recruit for him. It was decided to deploy an army corps before Paris and to muster the greatest possible number of national guardsmen and volunteers. On the 18th, M. le Duc de Berri† was named general of that army. Marshal Macdonald was placed in command under the prince.

But the organization of the volunteers and flying columns took several days. Every moment gave rise to a new danger. Bonaparte advanced quickly. Several regiments stationed along his route had gone over to him. Some had even taken possession of Burgundian towns in his name. One of them preceded him into Auxerre.

There was still a slim hope that the troops of the first military division, and those of the garrison in Paris, would remain loyal. An imminent danger averted by the loyalty of La Fère's commandant and the arrest of the traitors d'Erlon and Lallemand, seemed encouraging for the northern provinces. The Duc de Reggio,‡ deserted by the old guard, had managed to keep a tight rein on the other troops in his command. It was hoped to establish a reserve army under the command of the Duc de Trévise at Péronne, where the assembled troops would be less susceptible to blandishments. M. le Duc d'Orléans set out for that city.

---

†*Monsieur*'s younger son; the king's nephew.
‡Marshal Oudinot.

It was at this time that the king appeared before the nation's representatives, whose company he had willingly chosen at the first signs of national danger. His speech to the two Houses made a great impression in the capital, whose citizens responded with unanimous and heartfelt devotion to king and country. But the national guard, composed largely of family men, could not furnish enough volunteers for any real hope of resistance. General Dessolles advised intermixing citizens and soldiers, to keep the latter loyal, and reinforcing them with the king's household cavalry.

On the 17th, disastrous news: Marshal Ney, whom we all believed in pursuit of the rebels, had gone over to them; his infamous proclamation called upon the troops to share his dishonor. The town of Sens, where we had hoped to slow Napoleon's advance, declared itself incapable of resistance. The enemy was marching on Fontainebleau, and the troops in Paris stood mute, or showed only a sullen desire to abandon their flags.

This gloomy state of affairs rapidly degenerated into overt sedition. During the morning of the 19th we learned that there was not a single regiment defending Paris that could be counted on. So nothing remained to check Bonaparte's advance, and the only course left to the king was to retreat with his household troops. His Majesty, who had sent M. le Duc de Bourbon into the western provinces and invested M. le Duc d'Angoulême† with authority to command the armed

---

†*Monsieur*'s elder son; the king's nephew.

forces of the southern provinces, thought he would do best to fall back to the northern provinces, where frontier strongholds could serve as rallying points for his faithful subjects. The king left at midnight of the 19th and was followed an hour later by his household troops under the orders of *Monsieur* and the Duc de Berri.

Reaching Abbeville at five in the afternoon of the 20th, the king decided to await his troops there; but Marshal Macdonald, who caught up with him at noon on the 21st, persuaded the king that he must retreat yet farther. According to his account, His Majesty resolved to withdraw into Lille, and sent his household troops the order to join him there by the Amiens road.

On the 22d, an hour past noon, the king, preceded by the Duc de Tarente, entered Lille, where he was welcomed by lively demonstrations of love and loyalty from the citizenry. The Duc d'Orléans had preceded His Majesty, as had M. le Duc de Trévise, who believed it prudent to order the regional garrison back into the city. This last move, of which the king had not been advised, might well have compromised the proposed defensive scheme. If those troops had not entered the city, the national guard and household troops, with the support of the patriotic Lillois, might have secured this last haven on French soil for the king. But with a numerous and ill-deployed garrison that plan seemed most difficult of execution. Still, His Majesty persisted in the attempt. His presence had already roused the populace to heights of enthusiasm. An eager crowd swarmed after him, making strenuous efforts to inspire the soldiers by a constant chorus of "*Vive le roi!*" The troops, morose and stony, maintained a bleak silence, a disquieting omen of their impending defection. And indeed Marshal Mortier† told the king bluntly that he could not answer for the local troops. Queried about possible last resorts, he stated that it was not in his power to force the troops from their present positions.

In the midst of all this, the declaration issued in Vienna on March 15th, in the name of all the European powers, reached Lille. The king ordered it immediately distributed and posted, hoping (but vainly) to show the troops the dire consequences of their treason and the inevitable misfortunes it would bring down on the country.

On the 23d His Majesty learned that the Duc de Bassano,‡ in his capacity as Minister of the Interior, had forwarded Bonaparte's instructions to the prefect of Lille. That same day, an hour after noon, Marshal Mortier came to report to the secretary of the royal household that according to a widely believed rumor the Duc de Berri was about to arrive with the household troops and two Swiss regiments, and the local troops were on the point of mutiny; and that he urged the king to leave, in order to avoid the most frightful trouble; and that by personally escorting His Majesty outside the city gates he hoped to be able to control the garrison, but that he could not answer for it if the departure were delayed even an instant.

The king judged it best to order his household troops to proceed to Dunkirk, an order which was unfortunately not received. Unable

---

†Marshal Mortier was the Duc de Trévise (Treviso).

‡Hugues-Bernard Maret, a man of state and not a marshal. He served Napoleon loyally, yet later became a peer of France (that is, a member of the Upper House) under Louis-Philippe.

himself to go directly to that city, he made for Ostend. His Majesty left Lille at three o'clock, accompanied by Marshal Mortier and followed by M. le Duc d'Orléans. At the foot of the glacis† the Duc de Trévise felt it his duty to turn back, to prevent possible disorders by the garrison in his absence. M. le Duc d'Orléans also returned, finally leaving only several hours later. Marshal Macdonald did not part from the king until the gates of Menin, and to the very end gave His Majesty and the Duc de Trévise consoling proof that among the pride of the French army not everyone scoffed at the sanctity of a solemn oath, and the faith of a man of honor.

A unit of the Lille national guard and a detachment of the king's cavalry accompanied His Majesty to the border. Some of these latter, as well as several officers, refused to desert the king and accompanied him onto Belgian soil. The king proceeded to Ostend, hoping to make his way to Dunkirk as soon as his household troops occupied that city.

Meanwhile those hapless household troops, swelled by a crowd of volunteers of all ages and conditions, had followed the same road to Lille taken by the king. *Monsieur* and M. le Duc de Berri, still at the head of that gallant elite corps and sharing all its fatigues, rode in constant admiration of its steadfast heroism. Young men bearing arms for the first time, and old men making forced marches on foot over roads rendered almost impassible by heavy and continuous rains,

---

† An open slope outside a fortification or walled town, affording defenders clear view and unobstructed field of fire.

had flocked to that faithful band, undismayed by either the privations or the uncertainties of a journey rendered more perilous every moment by the defection of nearby garrisons. Lacking the orders not properly relayed from the king, and hearing that His Majesty had left Lille, the column struck directly for the border. Marshal Marmont, subordinate only to the princes, led them with a zeal and tactical skill that deserved better success; but some of these unfortunate troops, on foot and unable to keep up, slogging through muddy terrain that even the horses toiled painfully to cross, were forced to fall behind. *Monsieur*, fearing that their devotion to duty would expose them to useless danger, left them free to disband and retire. Surprised and surrounded in Béthune on orders received from Paris, they were not all able to disperse, so that the most *Monsieur* could hope was to rally stragglers at the border. In that hope he halted there.

At eight in the evening of the 25th, the king learned that *Monsieur* had arrived in Ypres; and news of the sore trials his household troops had suffered was added to the burden of melancholy that overwhelmed him.

In the midst of all these disasters His Majesty received some striking evidences of loyalty; but in a sense these only aggravated his sorrows. It was a decent and kindly nation that he left vulnerable to a misled and licentious soldiery; a nation of devoted and courageous servants of the crown, and he was unable even to stand and rally them. And to the qualities of unshakable constancy in many military leaders, the most distinguished of that whole army which the king still hoped to call his own, he could offer no recompense but the reward of esteem and encomium that France and posterity would one day bestow upon them.

After His Majesty's arrival in Ostend he learned from M. le Duc d'Orléans that an order to place him and all his princes under arrest had reached Marshal Mortier. Bearing a dispatch from Marshal Davoust including that order among others, a staff officer arrived in Lille, whence the king had already withdrawn; but the Duc de Trévise arranged matters so that its contents were not made public until M. le Duc d'Orléans had departed.

This account of the principal events of the brief and unfortunate period here outlined may convey some idea of the sudden and innumerable difficulties with which the king found himself beset. Never have so many unforeseen events, unfolding so rapidly, changed the face of a great monarchy; but never has a more striking conflict between the civil and military spirits burst upon a people. An important lesson for any nation so imprudent as to submit itself to a military government!*

Moreover, the simultaneous and almost universal defection of the army was, as we see, based on no principle that could long attach it

---

*This remark may imply to readers that the author assumes that a nation has the option of submitting to one government or another only when it is pleased to do so! Whatever the case, it is only too true that France's misfortunes offer important lessons. But it is not only great nations, it is also kings and princes, who ought to profit by them. It is essential that they and their courts teach the public the dangers of despotism and military rule, and the troubles which sooner or later ensue. Neither nations nor even modern armies wish for military despotism, and I am persuaded that in the present state of mankind's opinions and beliefs a wise constitutional system is the best means of strengthening a throne and preserving a nation from the despotism of soldiers and courtiers alike.

to the fate of the man whose dire influence leads it astray today. His tacit agreement with the army will shortly be broken by the reverses in store for him. It is surely not a Bonaparte proscribed, rejected, and soon overwhelmed by all Europe who seduced this credulous soldiery: it was the ravager of the world, who promised to share his booty with them. His prestige dissipated, Bonaparte will soon lose his sham power. It is that moment, when calm reflection succeeds the wild intoxication of monumental error, which the king awaits; and he awaits it with all the more impatience as he counts on a happy outcome.

23 March 1815

On March 23d, between seven and eight in the morning, the king and the Duc de Trévise came looking for me. As soon as he saw me, the king said, "Well, sir, I have not left, as you see."

"Sire," I answered, "I received the message Your Majesty deigned to send last night, to forewarn me."

"I had no wish," the king continued, "to flee from Lille like a thief in the night."

"Ah, Sire," I said to him, "the departure of a king is not the flight of a thief. And now it is day."

"I should prefer to remain in Lille."

"I hope that Your Majesty may be able to do so; but unfortunately every indication leads us to believe that it cannot be for long."

"That is what we shall see," said the king.

An incident later in the morning, between nine and ten, might have proved very troublesome. Some country folk appeared at one of the gates of Lille (the *porte de Béthune*) and reported to the soldiers of the guard that the Duc de Berri was on his way at the head of two thousand Swiss, and that he was not far off.* The news spread throughout the city, and its effect was unfortunate. The troops very nearly took up arms, very nearly donned tricolor cockades, and very nearly manned battle stations to greet the Duc de Berri and the Swiss with rifle fire and artillery. Luckily the Duc de Trévise was told of the rumor in time. He hastened to notify the king, who ordered him

---

*At that time the king's household, following the order sent by His Majesty from Abbeville, was indeed on its way to Lille, via Béthune.

to deny the rumor and to assure the garrison that his household troops, whose destination he had altered, were not marching on Lille. The garrison calmed down, and there were no repercussions.

Toward noon the king sent for me and his marshals, and had us ushered into his office. He told us simply that he had sent for us to inform us that he planned to leave at three o'clock; but he did not honor us with his reasons for that decision. *

"May I ask," I addressed him, "where Your Majesty plans to go?"

"I shall cross the border," he answered. "I see that I can remain no longer in Lille, and I had best resign myself to the inevitable."

"Sire," I replied, "I agree entirely that the king neither can nor should remain longer in Lille, and that the sooner Your Majesty leaves, the better; but the king may leave Lille without leaving France. Why abandon the plans for Dunkirk?"

"Ah, Dunkirk!" said the king. "It is twenty-five leagues to Dunkirk. I do not know if I could make my way by the direct route. And in any case, as my household troops are not yet there, it would be the same as here. I am not certain that they can reach Dunkirk. And after all, I shall be able to go on to Dunkirk as easily across the border as on this side, if I judge the matter correctly."

"Ah, Sire," I said to him, "Your Majesty should not deceive him-

---

*We had just learned that the prefect had received dispatches from the Duc de Bassano, whom Bonaparte had temporarily assigned to the duties of Minister of the Interior. But whether or not the king knew that, he did not mention it to us; and I myself still do not know the contents of those dispatches. Nor do I know whether they were the reason for the king's sudden decision to leave Lille, and to quit French soil, or any part of his reason.

self; the border is a Rubicon not so easily passed a second time, once it has been crossed."

"I see no reason why that should be so," the king told me. "I plan to make for Ostend, but I shall not embark for several days. I shall await news there, and we shall see."

After that exchange, Marshal Macdonald took the floor, and said to him in solemn tones, "Sire, I once swore loyalty to Napoleon, and I take pride in having been one of the last to leave him. I take similar pride in standing by Your Majesty until the very moment of departure from France; but I shall not follow Your Majesty out of the country. Outside France I should only be a useless burden to Your Majesty. I beg the king to accept my resignation, and to allow me to accompany him as far as the border. When I have once seen Your Majesty to safety, I shall return here and retire to my own estates."

Marshal Mortier spoke in the same vein to the king, whom he begged to accept his resignation; he intended, like Marshal Macdonald, to retire to his own home; and he asked that the king indicate what course of action he should follow in his command, once His Majesty had withdrawn.

The king answered, "You must act as circumstances dictate; I leave it to you entirely. If they oblige you to wear another cockade in your hat, do so; but you will keep mine always in your heart, and I am sure that you will wear it again when the time is right."

"And in my heart also," the Marshal replied, "I shall always keep the memory of Your Majesty's kindnesses."

Then I spoke, and asked the king what he wished me to do.

"Upon my word," the king said. "You may do whatever you think fit."

"Well then, Sire," I went on, "as Your Majesty leaves me such latitude, here is what I propose to do. I shall ride with the Duc de Trévise and escort Your Majesty as far as the glacis; then I shall return here, and stay as long as there is any hope that I may forward Your Majesty's cause by serving it here. I fear that will not be for long. When I am convinced that my efforts are of no use, I shall leave, and go immediately to England, to join my wife and children and await events."

"That is surely your best course," answered the king.

At three o'clock the king boarded his coach and we mounted our horses. A squadron of cavalry, commanded by a colonel of their regiment, escorted His Majesty. We heard shouts of *Vive le roi!* from the crowd gathered before His Majesty's house; but riding through the crowd we noted a certain uneasiness. On all sides they asked us whether the king was leaving Lille, and where he was going. We pretended not to hear, but those questions became very embarrassing when the king's coach halted; which happened twice—to repair broken traces—before we left the city. At the city gate more trouble delayed the king. The soldiers of the guard refused to open the gate. Marshal the Duc de Trévise lost patience with the officer of the day, and at his imposing and angry command the gate was opened. On the glacis, the Duc de Trévise and I took leave of the king. We returned to the city immediately. Marshal the Duc de Tarente accompanied the king as far as the border and then returned to Lille.

I had more meetings then with the two marshals, the generals, and the colonels, and it did not take me long to decide that there was nothing more for me to do here, and that further efforts would only compromise those who joined me in making them. I therefore decided to leave that night.

Only after I had come to that decision did I learn from Marshal the Duc de Trévise (he had, with the utmost delicacy, kept it not only from me but also from the king) that he had received a dispatch by semaphore from some fifteen leagues off, by which he was enjoined to arrest the king and any others of the House of Bourbon who might be in Lille. He told me besides that since the king's departure an aide-de-camp of Marshal Davoust* had appeared at the gates; that he had ordered the man admitted and brought before him; and had found him the bearer of orders to arrest the king, as well as myself. He added that he had detained this aide-de-camp; and begging me to ignore the whole incident, he requested me to stay in Lille just as long as I should have without knowledge of it. I had already a deep appreciation of the Duc's quality and held him in sincere affection; I had no need of this latest act of loyalty to do justice to the nobility of his character.

In leaving France without issuing positive orders to Marshal the Duc de Trévise and myself, the king had placed us in an awkward position with those whom we had previously commanded in his name. Unable to count on safety anywhere in northern France, hav-

*Marshal Davoust had just been named Minister of War by Bonaparte.

ing withdrawn to a foreign land, the king had tacitly acknowledged the impossibility of serious resistance in the region under my command, and, consequently of executing the orders I had previously issued. It seemed to me that before leaving, the king should have indicated his further intentions to the French people; but he did not do so.

He left France without setting forth a program; no general orders, no proclamation, no manifesto marked his departure, nothing to advise public officials in their new circumstances, or to lay out a line of conduct that he desired them to follow; so that for them as well as for all army officers there remained no guide but their patriotism and sense of duty.

It is true that the first number of the *Journal universel*, published in Ghent on April 14th, contained two general orders from the king dated March 23d at Lille; but these had not previously appeared, and I persist in my conviction that they were not issued at Lille. If they had been, I believe it was the king's duty to announce immediately to all interested parties (which means really the whole of France) the ordinances by which he would later claim the right to judge, or to see judged, their actions. It is common knowledge that on March 23d the king could have proclaimed, and had published in Lille, these two general orders or such others as he deemed appropriate, and it is equally well known that the king did no such thing, though that formal procedure was absolutely indispensable if we were to claim the right to begin executing those orders as of the date of their publication, three weeks later, in the gazette at Ghent.

I cannot believe that if those orders had really been issued at Lille, the king would not have communicated them to Marshals the Duc de Trévise and Duc de Tarente, and to myself, when we asked what final orders he had for us at his departure. I have already said that he answered the Duc de Trévise, "You must act as circumstances dictate," and even foreseeing that events might force the marshal to substitute the tricolor cockade for the white, he had added, "do so; and whatever cockade you wear in your hat, I know that you will keep mine always in your heart, and I am sure that you will wear it again when the time is right." It would have been impossible for the king to make such a statement if the two general orders had been issued before his departure from Lille, and it seems to me also impossible that he would not have communicated them to us, if they had been in existence.

With the king gone from Lille, and from France, without leaving any orders or any instructions whatever, either for the marshal or for me, he had in effect placed us in command, as he had replaced neither of us. I could not yield that command and withdraw from French soil without informing my subordinates of the course events were forcing upon me; I owed it to them all the more as I had previously given them specific orders implementing a plan no longer feasible. It was consequently my duty to cancel those orders and to warn them that I was abandoning the plan, which would at least free them of the burden of meaningless obligations. It has been rumored that I absolved all commanders of fortified cities of their oath of fealty to the king; nothing could be more false, and nothing better proves the falsity of the assertion than the following letter, which I wrote to Marshal the Duc de Trévise in appointing him commander-in-chief; and also the circular I addressed to all commanders of fortified towns who were under my orders, this being the document on which I presume some have tried to base that slander.

To Monsieur le Duc de Trévise

Lille, 23 March 1815

I have just appointed you, my dear Marshal, to the full command I should have been so happy to share with you in the northern provinces. I am too good a Frenchman to sacrifice the interests of France merely because fresh difficulties force me to leave the country. I go to bury myself in retirement and oblivion. The king being no longer in France, I can no longer give you orders in his name, and all I can do now is to release you from the obligation to execute any orders I have previously issued to you, and to urge that you do whatever your sound judgment and honest patriotism suggest is best for the interests of France and most appropriate to the duties you have to perform. Be kind enough to transmit the attached letters to all commanders of fortified towns formerly under my orders, so that I may carry into this new exile to which I consign myself the satisfaction of having done my duty toward them, as I am quite sure they would have done theirs toward me if circumstances had permitted. Adieu, my dear Marshal—my heart contracts as I write the word; remain my friend wherever fortune leads me, † and count on me always as yours; I shall never forget

197

---

† He did. In 1835 while accompanying Louis-Philippe to a review, he was among those killed by a bomb aimed at the king.

what I saw of you during the too brief time we served together; I admire your noble loyalty and your staunch character as much as I esteem and love you; and it is with all my heart, my dear Marshal, that I wish you all the good fortune you so well deserve, and which I yet hope for you.

Your affectionate,
Louis-Philippe d'Orléans

At the same time I wrote the following circular to all general officers in command of fortified towns in the 16th Military District:

Lille, 23 March 1815

I have to inform you, my dear General, that as in our present unfortunate circumstances the king has resolved to leave France, at three o'clock this afternoon I release you from all obligation to execute orders conveyed to you by me in his name, and I rely on your judgment and your patriotism to guide you in doing what you think most appropriate to the interests of France and your own duty.

Communicate the provisions of this letter to the town-majors of your command, and to the troops under your orders.

Louis-Philippe d'Orléans

Having completed all this, I had only to make final arrangements about my aides-de-camp. Baron Albert, who was a lieutenant general, a family man, and the owner of properties in France, could not and should not think of leaving to follow me to a foreign country. Colonel Athalin and Raoul de Montmorency proposed to come with me and share my lot; I was moved by their proposal, and would have been much consoled to accept if, for one thing, long and sad experience had not taught me how uncertain my lot was and if, for another, I had not always discouraged emigration on principle.

Besides, Athalin was a colonel of genius, and his career was infinitely preferable to anything I might have offered him outside France; and Raoul was an only son who must not jeopardize either his family or his fortune. So I declined their offer, great as was my sorrow at parting from them.

My other aides-de-camp were in different situations. The name and properties of the succession to which Camille de Saint-Aldegonde was heir were in Belgium, so it was natural and even preferable that he leave France. Thibaud de Montmorency had good and sufficient reason to take the same course, as did M. de Chabot; so I could not advise them to do otherwise, and decided to take them with me.

I was deeply saddened also at parting from Marshal Macdonald, for whom I long cherished a great friendship.

24 March 1815: My Departure from France

Finally, on March 24th at three in the morning, I boarded a coach with my sister, Madame de Montjoye, and Marshal the Duc de Trévise, who insisted on escorting me outside the gates, where I bade him farewell. Those of my aides-de-camp who were remaining in France followed me as far as the border, where they left me, as did the detachment of cuirassiers which had been my escort since our arrival at Lille.

I arrived in Tournai at daybreak. I wrote immediately to the king, informing him of my departure from France and of the great service that Marshal the Duc de Trévise had just rendered him. I then hastened on my way, to join my wife and children in England.

After the battle of Waterloo, in June of 1815, Napoleon was exiled to Saint Helena, where he spent the rest of his life. Louis XVIII was restored to the throne of France and reigned as a constitutional monarch—reactionary, moderately intelligent, a pleasant, fat, lazy man at whose court most of Napoleon's marshals mingled freely with the bluebloods. Still, there were limits; Louis-Philippe was a liberal, and so outspoken in the house of peers that in the autumn of 1815 he was exiled once more to England, for two years.

Charles X (whom we have met as Monsieur) succeeded in 1824, a foolish and haughty man, an extreme reactionary who believed in the divine right of kings. He abdicated (and was deposed for good measure) during the inevitable revolutionary turmoil of 1830.

The legislature invited Louis-Philippe to take the throne. He was "a prince devoted to the principles of the Revolution," he had "carried the tricolor under fire," and would be a "citizen king." He was at first popular, "the bourgeois king," simple and democratic; the Palais-Royal was open to casual visitors and ordinary citizens. After all, Louis-Philippe had roamed the American frontier.

Still, he was a Bourbon and a king. He might scorn pomp and circumstance, and welcome the support of the middle classes, but his ambitions were dynastic. Perhaps after so turbulent a life, so many confiscations and restorations, exiles and returns, wars and peaces, his deepest desire was for stability, order, hierarchy, even at the expense of liberty. The citizen king responded to conflicts of power and policy by becoming more the king and less the citizen; his American journey receded into the past.

In the revolution of 1848 he was himself deposed. (The Bourbon and the bourgeois merged perfectly in his protest: "I shall never abdicate—at least not until I have consulted my wife.") He and his queen stole out of the Tuileries by a back gate and

201

went in disguise to Honfleur, where they hid in a gardener's cottage until the British consul at Le Havre could smuggle them across the Channel, ironically as "Mr and Mrs Smith." In England—the last exile—they lived quietly and comfortably, sadly and aristocratically, as the Count and Countess of Neuilly, at Claremont, an estate placed at their disposal by Queen Victoria.

In 1850, over half a century after his American journey, Louis-Philippe died at seventy-six.

S.B.